Indian FOOD & FOLKLORE

Indian FOOD & FOLKLORE

LAUREL GLEN

Published in the United States by
Laurel Glen Publishing
5880 Oberlin Drive, Suite 400
San Diego, CA 92121-4794
http://www.advmkt.com

ISBN 1-57145-650-3
Library of Congress Cataloging-in-Publication Data available
upon request.

1 2 3 4 5   99 00 01 02 03

Printed in China by Toppan Printing Co., (H.K.) Ltd

Editor Cara Frost
Copy Editor Jo Lethaby
Art Director Keith Martin
Designer Claire Harvey
Production Controller Katherine Hockley

Contributors
Photographer Ian Wallace
Home Economist Eliza Baird
Stylist Clare Hunt
Picture Researcher Liz Fowler
Indexer Pamela Le Gassick

North American edition
Publisher Allen Orso
Managing Editor JoAnn Padgett
Project Editor Elizabeth McNulty

NOTES
Standard level spoon measurements are used in all recipes.
1 tablespoon = one 15 ml spoon
1 teaspoon = one 5 ml spoon

Both imperial and metric measurements have been given in all
recipes. Use one set of measurements only and not a mixture of both.

Eggs should be medium unless otherwise stated.

Ovens should be preheated to the specified temperature; if using a
convection oven, follow the manufacturer's instructions for adjusting
the time and temperature.

Acknowledgments
AKG, London: Paul Almasy 6, 70
Corbis UK Ltd: Hulton-Getty Collection 8, 9, 18, 31, 51,
141 / Karan Kapoor 38 / Earl Kowall 41, 108 / Craig Lovell
11, 23, 62, 123 / Hans George Roth 119 / Bradley Smith
124 / Nevada Wier 35
Octopus Publishing Group Ltd: Ian Wallace 14, 15, 21, 25,
29, 33, 37, 43, 47, 53, 57, 61, 65, 69, 73, 75, 81, 85, 89, 93,
97, 99, 103, 107, 113, 117, 121, 129, 131, 134, 139
Robert Harding Picture Library: 3 insert, 59, 77, 87, 100,
125, 133 / Jeremy Bright 82 /Alain Evrard 110 / T. Gervis
45 / Michael Short 83 / Claude Wilson 49 / J.H.C. Wilson
17, 30, 115
Image Bank: Carlos Navajas 12 / Anne Rippy 78 / Harald
Sand 54 / Stephen Wilkes 5, 26
Tony Stone Images: Steward Cohen 66 / Will Curtis 1, 144 /
Nicholas DeVore 7, 104 / David Hanson 94 / Paul Harris 16
/ Gavin Hellier 126 / Chris Noble 136 / Martin Salter 10 /
David Sutherland 3 main picture, 91

Jacket credits
Will Curtis jacket wrap-around / T. Gervis front flap top /
David Hanson back flap top
Octopus Publishing Group Ltd: Ian Wallace front jacket insert

Contents

introduction

India is such a vast country that the style of cooking varies enormously from region to region. Geography—climate and soil—and local produce have played a big part in forming regional culinary traditions. Religious groups have modified the regional cuisines even further to suit their own beliefs and restrictions. History, too, has had a role, and outsiders have all left their mark on Indian food and cooking—from the Muslim Moguls with their Persian-style cuisine, to the Catholic Portuguese, who ruled Goa on the Indian west coast for four centuries, and further to the British colonials of the Raj who also left dishes in their wake.

RELIGION

Nearly 85 percent of India's population is Hindu, while another 11 percent is Muslim. Other faiths account for the rest of the population and include Jainism, Buddhism, Sikhism, Christianity, and Zoroastrianism. Many of the various religions have had a role in shaping Indian cooking. Hindus, for example, have a religious fondness for bright red and yellow, which is reflected in their use of saffron and turmeric. In the past, "impure" Hindu dishes could be purified by pouring ghee (clarified butter) over the top. Hindus offer food and drink to their gods and goddesses to show devotion, and some stone figures have become so coated with melted ghee and turmeric by pilgrims that they have lost their features. The gods are known to have their preferences—elephant-headed Ganesh, for example, favors sweets flavored with cardamom. Hindus regard the cow as sacred and therefore do not eat beef, while Muslims will not eat pork. Jains are strictly vegetarian and believe everything possesses life. Some Jains are so orthodox that they refrain from eating beets and tomatoes because the color is similar to that of blood. They also exclude from their diet root vegetables such as garlic, onions, carrots, potatoes, and ginger because the roots have a potential to grow.

SPICES

Bearing in mind the regional differences in Indian cooking, the common denominator must surely be the spices. Certainly, Indian cooking is characterized by the use of a

greater range of spices than almost any other cuisine. While the food is always spicy in flavor, it is not necessarily hot. The heat in Indian food, in fact, comes from hot chili peppers, which were only introduced to Asia in the 16th century by the Portuguese who had discovered them in the New World.

Indian cooks may use the spices whole, they may fry or roast them, or perhaps grind them with water or vinegar to make a paste. Each technique draws out a completely different flavor from the same spice. In this way, a group of spices can add ever greater variety to a diet of staple ingredients.

In the ancient Indian Ayurvedic (*science of life*) system of medicine, spices are used for more than just flavor. They are prescribed in order to alleviate or prevent medical problems, enhance mood, or trigger a physical reaction. Some are valued for their vitamin content and others, such as fenugreek, asafoetida, and fresh ginger, for their use in combating flatulence in a diet based on pulses and starchy vegetables.

CURRY & CURRY POWDER
The word "curry" is thought to be a corruption of the Tamil, or southern Indian word, *karhi*, which means sauce. Alternatively, it may have come from *karhai* or *karahi*, a commonly used two-handled Indian cooking vessel

similar to a wok. The curries first encountered by Europeans, from whom we have written accounts, seem to have been of a fairly liquid consistency, usually described as a broth or soup, poured over rice.

Throughout the days of the Raj, the term "curry" evolved as a loose description of any Indian food cooked in a sauce. The early merchants and soldiers who visited India and enjoyed the richly spiced Indian dishes were keen to introduce the flavor when they returned home. Demand for a commercial curry powder developed over decades, and such spice mixtures have slowly become better in quality, blending different spices according to the seasonings used in different regions. However, curry powder as such is not a traditional authentic ingredient in Indian cooking and certainly does not exist in

India. Most traditional households use individual spices, which are freshly ground and mixed as and when needed. The various blends used reflect the availability of the spices and the climate of the region to which they are accredited. Spice blends from the hotter regions contain more fiery chili flavors, for example, while mixtures from cooler, northern climes usually concentrate on more subtly fragrant flavors.

EARLY INDIAN CULTURE
It is known from archaeological evidence that a highly sophisticated, urbanized culture, the Indus civilization, dominated the northwest part of the subcontinent from about 2600 to 2000 BC. An Aryan or "Indo-European" civilization from the Eurasian steppes, dominated by peoples with linguistic affinities to groups in Iran and Europe,

moved into India from about 1700 BC onward. They occupied the northwest first, in what is now the Punjab, and then north-central India, and subsequently spread southward and eastward at the expense of various indigenous groups. The Aryans' cultural and religious beliefs, based on their ancient Vedic scriptures, were mixed with those of the existing population and gradually laid the foundations of Indian society and the Hindu faith, with its caste system and belief in reincarnation.

The status of the cow

With the arrival of the Aryans, livestock, cattle in particular, assumed greater importance, and they appear to have introduced a heavy dependence on dairy produce. The Aryans' diet included milk and curds—the latter being a popular food in a hot climate where its slight tartness was refreshing—and they cooked with ghee (clarified butter), which unlike fresh butter can be kept for months, even in a hot climate.

The Aryans brought their own cattle with them but these were gradually superseded by the native Indian breed, which was better adapted to the climate. The latter gave less milk, however, and as the indigenous people adopted dairy products with enthusiasm, demand probably outstripped supply. It therefore became necessary to protect the cow with the fullest sanctity of religious law. This belief in the sacredness of the cow and dairy products slowly diffused throughout the whole of the subcontinent.

In time, the law against cattle slaughter was relaxed and by about 700 BC, it was generally accepted that cattle could be killed in the name of hospitality or in sacrifice to the gods and spirits. However, the increasing pressure on farmers for their valuable draft and milk animals by priests demanding cattle for ritual sacrifice provoked a strong social reaction and led to the emergence of two new religions—Buddhism and Jainism. Both sects opposed ritual sacrifice; they believed in the sanctity of all life and advocated vegetarianism. So influential was their anti-slaughter campaign that by the first century BC even the Brahmin priests of the orthodox Vedic faith had come round again and all three religions agreed that the cow was sacred.

EXTERNAL INFLUENCES ON COOKING

In the early centuries of the first millennium AD it appears that Indians ate two meals a day. The daily diet depended on the part of the country in which people lived. Wheat and barley could be grown in winter only in the south but at almost any time of the year in the cooler parts of the north. Rice was the standard crop on southern plains where there was irrigation. Gourds, peas, beans, and lentils were found throughout the country and sugar cane, tamarind, and mango were widely grown.

Although rice, local spices, vegetables, and fish were the base of south Indian cooking,

the food was subject to many outside influences arriving by sea. To the repertoire of spices already used—pepper, cardamom, and ginger—coriander and cumin were introduced to India's Malabar coast from the eastern Mediterranean via trade with the Arab world and Rome. On the other side of the subcontinent, the east-facing Coromandel coast had contact with the islands of Asia and with China, and imported from there nutmeg, mace, and cloves.

While the Indian coasts received visitors by sea, in northwestern India, foreign contact came overland, through the passes of the Hindu Kush, in a succession of invasions and infiltrations of ideas, attitudes, and techniques over thousands of years. Aryan, Persian, Greek, and Central Asian influences were all absorbed into the heritage of the Indus Valley civilization to produce a mixed culture. Because the land was fertile and many of the influences nomadic, meat was more commonly eaten here than anywhere else in India.

The arrival of Islam

Islam, too, came from the northwest, brought to India by successive Arab, Turkish, and Persian invaders from the early eighth century AD onward. The first Muslims brought with them their everyday foods and cooking methods, but it was the establishment of a Muslim imperial power in India in the 16th century—the Moguls—that had many far-reaching effects on both Indian society and food.

At the court of the Moguls a new haute cuisine was introduced, a style of cooking derived from the Persians. Kebabs, pilaf or pilau dishes of

rice with shredded meat, the technique of mixing fruits into meat dishes, the use of almonds and almond milk, rose petals, rosewater, and the garnishing of all kinds of food with fragile strips of tissue beaten out of pure gold and silver (varq) were all absorbed into the Indian cuisine. Although Islam allowed Muslims to eat beef, their cuisine was based mainly on mutton and chicken, and nonvegetarian Hindus were therefore able to adopt it easily. The later Moguls made generous use of the chilies first introduced by the Portuguese.

It was in the north, the heartland of Mogul rule, that Muslim food became most common. Even today, the cooking of the Punjab has almost as many links with the food of the Near East as with that of traditional India. One innovation that did spread from northern India throughout the whole subcontinent was the Muslim addiction to sweets. Confections of all kinds, made from sugar alone or sugar with coconut, rice flour, or with almonds, became immensely popular, as did sweet desserts such as *jallebi*.

EUROPEAN INFLUENCES

After the arrival in India of the Portuguese navigator, Vasco da Gama, in 1498 and the subsequent establishment of European maritime supremacy, India was exposed to more influences arriving by sea, lured by the trade in spices. Thus with the arrival of the English, French, Portuguese, Dutch, and Danish there began the development of Hindu-Muslim-European

cuisine, now simply known as "Indian."

The Portuguese brought from the New World chili and capsicum peppers, tomatoes, cashew nuts, pineapple, and papaya. The British introduced Northern European vegetables to India such as cabbages and broad and runner beans, which became well integrated into the Indian diet. Punjabi-Muslim food probably suffered the least at the hand of external influences because such curries were already based on meat and were therefore less adapted and altered by the meat-eating foreigners than were vegetarian curries.

European incursions into the subcontinent culminated in the attempted control of the region by the British East India Company and eventual absorption of India by the British Empire. Before this was achieved, however, British disregard for Indian religious beliefs was the catalyst for the Indian Mutiny of 1857. The mutiny was set in motion by the introduction of the new Enfield rifle, the cartridges for which were partially coated with grease and had to be bitten open before loading. Rumors flew through the ranks of the Indian *sepoys* that the grease was either beef or pork fat. For a caste Hindu to bite on the fat of the sacred cow was an inconceivable sin; to a Muslim, the fat of the unclean pig was insufferable pollution.

The Raj produced some unique Anglo-Indian results, one example of which is Worcestershire sauce. It is one of the few pungent sauces to have survived from its 19th-century heyday, and its recipe is a well-guarded secret, containing typically Indian ingredients that include tamarind, shallots, garlic, and spices such as cardamom and ginger.

When British rule came to an end in 1947, the subcontinent was partitioned along religious lines into two separate countries—India with a majority of Hindus, and Pakistan with a majority of Muslims. The eastern part of Pakistan later gained independence as Bangladesh. India remains ethnically diverse today, containing the many different religious sects, castes, and tribes, and major and minor linguistic groups, the existence of which still contribute to the considerable regional variations in Indian cuisine.

REGIONAL DIFFERENCES

Today, people tend to consume two or three meals per day depending on income. The bulk of almost all meals is whatever the regional staple might be—rice throughout most of the east and south, flat wheat bread like chapati in the north and northwest. This is usually supplemented with *dhal* (a pulse dish), a vegetable dish, possibly a meat dish, a bowl of yogurt or a yogurt relish, and a freshly prepared chutney or small, relish-like salad dish.

As a general rule, foods tend to be hotter the further south you go in India. In more detail, the different regions in the country can be characterized as follows.

Northern India

The subtly spiced Punjabi and Kashmiri styles of cooking in

northern India owe much to the sophistication of the cooks at the luxurious courts of the Moguls, who came from Persia in the 16th century. The Punjab is particularly famous for its tandoori cooking and for its sweets. The Punjabis tend to consume wheat in preference to rice, while Kashmiri cooking is known for its meat cuisine. Ghee is the most commonly used cooking medium.

Southern India

The south is the stronghold of the Hindus. The Brahmins, monitors of the Hindu faith, taught nonviolence, advocated vegetarianism, and declared the cow a sacred animal. The staple foods in the south are therefore vegetables and rice. Mustard oil, with its slightly sweet flavor, is the commonly used cooking medium, and coconut, coconut milk, and tamarind are widely used. Curries from this part of India, which include the fierce vindaloos, are thin and fiery and use plenty of chilies. Curry leaves and mustard seeds are the great southern spices, and fenugreek and roasted pulses provide extra nutrition in the diet.

Eastern India

This region, which encompasses Bengal and Bihar, has good access to rivers and the sea, so fish is an important part of the local diet. Mustard oil is again the principal cooking medium, and foods are spiced with mustard, cumin, anise, and fenugreek seeds. The easterners are particularly well known for their delicious sweets and savory snacks.

Western India

The cuisine of western India is derived principally from Goa and Bombay. Food from Goa, once colonized by the Portuguese, tends to be hot and spicy and uses a lot of coconut milk, vinegar, and tamarind juice. Bombay is famed for its chutneys and pickles, its fruit ice creams, and its refreshing cold drinks made with fruit juices and yogurt, known as *sharbats*.

Central India

The cuisine from central India is dominated by the Mogul influence of the north but it also has certain southern touches and adaptations—for example cashew nuts and coconut have replaced Turkish walnuts and Persian almonds. The Moguls ate beef, unlike the Hindus, and their culinary influence is particularly evident in many regional meat dishes.

snacks
&small dishes

Snacking plays a major part in the average Indian diet. Goodies to be nibbled are often wrapped in newspaper cones or tea towel bundles. The best place to eat samosas is undoubtedly right on the street where the odors from a samosa maker are too overwhelming to resist. All kinds of kebabs are also sold at open street stalls. Other popular snacks are grilled cashew nuts and lentil and eggplant fritters served with yogurt sauce or chutney.

Pakora

1 cup gram flour (besan)
1 teaspoon salt
½ teaspoon chili powder
⅔ cup water
2 green chilies, finely chopped
1 tablespoon finely chopped
    cilantro (fresh coriander)
1 teaspoon melted butter or ghee
2 onions, cut into rings
oil, for deep-frying
8 small fresh spinach leaves
2–3 potatoes, parboiled and sliced
whole red chilies, fried, to garnish

Pakora are made of onion rings, spinach leaves, and parboiled potatoes, which are dipped into a spicy batter and deep-fried until they are crisp and golden.

1 Sift the flour, salt, and chili powder into a bowl. Stir in sufficient water to make a thick batter and beat well until smooth. Leave to stand for 30 minutes.

2 Stir the chilies and cilantro into the batter, then add the melted butter or ghee. Drop in the onion rings to coat thickly with batter.

3 Heat the oil in a deep pan to 375°F, or until a cube of bread browns in 30 seconds. Drop in the onion rings and deep-fry until crisp and golden. Remove from the pan with a slotted spoon, drain on kitchen paper and keep warm.

4 Dip the spinach leaves into the batter and deep-fry in the same way, adding more oil to the pan if necessary.

5 Finally, repeat the process with the potato slices. Serve the pakora hot, garnished with whole fried chilies.

Serves 4
Preparation time: 15 minutes, plus standing
Cooking time: 20 minutes

Cook's Note
Besan, or gram flour, is ground from channa dhal lentils, which come from the chickpea family. (When split and skinned, these lentils are bright yellow and resemble split peas.) Gram flour is often used in Indian cooking instead of wheat flour and is a particularly useful ingredient when cooking for people who are allergic to gluten, a component of all wheat products. It is available in larger supermarkets and Indian specialty grocers.

Spiced Scrambled Eggs

1 tablespoon butter
1 onion, finely chopped
2 green chilies, finely chopped
8 eggs, lightly beaten with
  2 tablespoons water
1 tablespoon finely chopped
  cilantro
salt

Scrambled eggs, flavored with chilies and cilantro.

1 Heat the butter in a large frying pan, add the onion and fry until deep golden. Add the chilies and fry for 30 seconds, then add the beaten eggs, cilantro, and salt to taste.
2 Cook, stirring, until the eggs are scrambled and set. Serve hot.

Serves 4
Preparation time: 5–10 minutes
Cooking time: 5 minutes

Lamb Kebab

A combination of ground lamb and flavorings. Traditionally, kebabs would be speared on presoaked wooden skewers and grilled.

1 Combine all the ingredients together very thoroughly in a large bowl and season with salt and pepper to taste. Using your hands, roll the mixture into 8–12 thin sausage shapes.

2 Place the kebabs under a preheated moderate grill and cook for about 10 minutes, turning several times. Serve garnished with chopped parsley and onion.

Serves 4
Preparation time: 10–15 minutes
Cooking time: 10 minutes

1 lb. ground lamb
2 tablespoons finely chopped
    celery leaves
2 tablespoons chopped parsley
2 onions, finely chopped
1 teaspoon turmeric
salt and pepper

TO GARNISH:
chopped parsley
finely chopped onion

"The food that man eats and his universe must be in harmony."
Vedic teaching

Vegetable Samosas

PASTRY:
1 cup all-purpose flour
¼ teaspoon salt
1 tablespoon ghee or butter
2–3 tablespoons water
FILLING:
1 tablespoon vegetable oil
1 teaspoon mustard seeds
1 small onion, finely chopped
2 green chilies, finely chopped
¼ teaspoon turmeric
1 teaspoon finely chopped fresh
    ginger
⅔ cup frozen peas
⅔ cup cooked potatoes, diced
½ tablespoon chopped cilantro
1 tablespoon lemon juice
oil, for deep-frying
salt

1 Sift the flour and salt into a mixing bowl. Rub in the ghee or butter until the mixture resembles breadcrumbs. Add the water and knead to a smooth dough. Cover and chill.
2 Meanwhile, prepare the filling. Heat the oil in a pan and add the mustard seeds. Leave for a few seconds until they start to pop, then add the onion and fry until golden. Add the chilies, turmeric, ginger, and salt to taste and fry for 3 minutes. If the mixture sticks to the pan, add ½ tablespoon water and stir. Add the peas, stir, and cook for 2 minutes. Add the potatoes and cilantro, stir and cook for 1 minute. Stir in the lemon juice and leave to cool slightly.
3 Divide the pastry into 8 pieces. Dust with flour and roll each piece into a thin circle, then cut each circle in half. Fold each semicircle into a cone and brush the seam with water to seal.
4 Fill the cones with a spoonful of the filling. Dampen the top edge and seal firmly. Heat the oil for deep-frying in a deep pan to 375°F, or until a cube of bread browns in 30 seconds. Deep-fry the samosas until crisp and golden. Serve hot or warm.

Serves 4
Preparation time: 15 minutes
Cooking time: 35 minutes

Meat Samosas

Samosas are deep-fried pastries stuffed with vegetables or meat, herbs, and spices.

1 Sift the flour and salt into a mixing bowl. Rub in the ghee or butter until the mixture resembles breadcrumbs. Add the water and knead thoroughly to a very smooth dough. Cover and chill while preparing the filling.

2 Heat the oil in a pan, add the onion and garlic and fry until golden. Add the chili and chili powder and fry for 3 minutes. Stir in the meat and cook until well browned. Add the tomato, chopped cilantro, and salt to taste and simmer gently for 20 minutes, until the meat is tender and the mixture is dry. Skim off any fat, stir well and leave to cool slightly.

3 Divide the pastry into 8 pieces. Dust with flour and roll each piece into a thin circle, then cut each circle in half. Fold each semicircle into a cone and brush the seam with water to seal.

4 Fill the cones with a spoonful of the filling, taking care not to overfill them. Dampen the top edge and seal firmly. Heat the oil for deep-frying in a deep pan to 375°F, or until a cube of bread browns in 30 seconds. Deep-fry the samosas until crisp and golden. Serve hot or warm.

Serves 4

Preparation time: 15 minutes
Cooking time: 35 minutes

PASTRY:
1 cup all-purpose flour
¼ teaspoon salt
1–2 tablespoons ghee or butter
2–3 tablespoons water

FILLING:
1 tablespoon vegetable oil
1 small onion, finely chopped
1 garlic clove, crushed
1 green chili, finely chopped
½ teaspoon chili powder
½ lb. ground beef
1 medium tomato, skinned and chopped
1 tablespoon chopped cilantro
oil, for deep-frying
salt

Stuffed Peppers

5 tablespoons vegetable oil
1 onion, finely chopped
2 teaspoons ground coriander
1 teaspoon ground cumin
½ teaspoon chili powder
¾ lb. ground beef
3 tablespoons long-grain rice,
    cooked
4 large green or red peppers
14 oz. canned tomatoes
salt
sprigs of cilantro, to garnish

1 Heat 3 tablespoons of the oil in a pan, add the onion, and fry until golden. Add the spices and cook for 2 minutes. Add the minced beef and fry, stirring, until browned. Add the rice and salt to taste and cook for 2 minutes. Remove from the heat and leave to cool.
2 Slice the peppers lengthwise and discard the seeds and cores. Fill the pepper shells with the meat mixture.
3 Heat the remaining oil in a pan just large enough to hold the peppers. Place the peppers in the pan. Pour a little of the canned tomato juice into each pepper and the remaining juice and tomatoes into the pan, seasoning with salt to taste. Bring to simmering point, cover and cook for about 25 minutes, until the peppers are tender. Pour the remaining tomatoes over the peppers and serve, garnished with cilantro sprigs.

Serves 4
Preparation time: 10 minutes
Cooking time: 40 minutes

"Food without hospitality is medicine."
Tamil proverb

Stuffed Cabbage Leaves

1 cabbage
5 tablespoons vegetable oil
1 onion, chopped
½ inch piece fresh ginger, chopped
1 teaspoon turmeric
1 lb. lean ground lamb
¾ cup long-grain rice
2 tomatoes, skinned and chopped
grated rind and juice of 2 lemons
2 teaspoons sugar
½ cup water
salt and pepper

1 Hollow out the stem end of the cabbage with a sharp knife. Place the cabbage in a large pan, cover with water and bring to the boil. Remove from the heat, cover the pan and leave to stand for 15 minutes. Drain.

2 Heat 2 tablespoons of the oil in another pan, add the onion and fry until soft. Add the ginger and turmeric and fry gently for 1 minute. Add the ground lamb and fry briefly until brown. Cool slightly, then stir in the rice, tomatoes, lemon rind and juice, and sugar. Mix well and season with salt and pepper to taste.

3 Carefully remove 12 inner leaves from the cabbage. Lay them flat on a work surface and divide the meat mixture between the 12 leaves, gently squeezing out and reserving any liquid. Fold each leaf into a little package.

4 Heat the remaining oil in a large frying pan. Lay the cabbage rolls in one layer in the pan as close together as possible. Pour over the reserved liquid from the filling and the measured water. Bring to simmering point, cover and cook for about 30 minutes.

5 If the liquid has not evaporated, increase the heat and cook, uncovered, for a few minutes. Lower the heat, turn the rolls, cover and cook for another 5 minutes before serving.

Serves 4–6
Preparation time: 30 minutes
Cooking time: 50–55 minutes

Chili Fry

1 Heat the oil in a frying pan, add the onion and fry until soft. Add the ground coriander, turmeric, ginger, and chili and fry over a low heat for 5 minutes. If the mixture becomes dry, add 1 tablespoon of water to the pan.

2 Add the strips of steak, increase the heat and cook, stirring, until browned all over. Add the chopped pepper, cover and simmer gently for 5–10 minutes, until the meat is tender. Add the tomatoes, lemon juice, and salt to taste and cook, uncovered, for 2–3 minutes—the dish should be rather dry. Serve with lemon wedges.

Serves 4
Preparation time: 15 minutes
Cooking time: 25 minutes

4 tablespoons vegetable oil
1 large onion, finely chopped
½ teaspoon ground coriander
½ teaspoon turmeric
1 inch piece fresh ginger, finely chopped
1 chili, chopped
1 lb frying steak, cut into strips about 1 x ½ inch
1 green or red pepper, cored, deseeded, and roughly chopped
2 tomatoes, quartered
4 tablespoons lemon juice
salt
lemon wedges, to serve

Chicken Tikka

⅔ cup plain yogurt
1 tablespoon grated fresh ginger
2 garlic cloves, crushed
1 teaspoon chili powder
1 tablespoon ground coriander
½ teaspoon salt
4 tablespoons lemon juice
2 tablespoons vegetable oil
1½ lb chicken breasts, skinned and
    boned

TO GARNISH:
lemon or lime wedges, lightly fried
1 red onion, diced

A mild dish made with chicken which is marinated with yogurt, ginger, and chili before being grilled.

1 Mix all the ingredients except the chicken together in a bowl. Cut the chicken into cubes, and drop into the marinade. Cover and leave in the refrigerator overnight.
2 Thread the pieces of chicken onto four metal or presoaked wooden skewers and cook under a preheated hot grill for 5–6 minutes, turning frequently.
3 The chicken can be left on the skewers or removed and arranged on individual serving plates. Serve garnished with fried lemon or lime wedges and diced red onion.

Serves 4
Preparation time: 10–15 minutes, plus marinating
Cooking time: 5–6 minutes

"The food earned by the plow is sweeter than that obtained by serving others."
Tamil Proverb

lamb, beef, & pork

Despite the fact that Indians only small amounts of meat, livestock-raising plays an important role in agriculture, and India has by far the largest bovine population of any country in the world. Cattle and buffalo provide milk and a source of meat for those Indians for whom beef-eating is not taboo. The Hindus and Muslims of India do not generally eat pork but Indian Christians do, hence the Goan-style dishes, which often include pork.

Stew with Potatoes and Peas

4 tablespoons vegetable oil
2 onions, finely chopped
2 teaspoons ground coriander
½ teaspoon turmeric
I inch piece fresh ginger, finely
    chopped
I chili, finely chopped
I heaped teaspoon garam masala
I lb. ground beef
½ lb. small potatoes, quartered
2 cups peas
salt

This is a relatively mild ground beef and vegetable curry.

1 Heat the oil in a frying pan, add the onions, and cook until soft. Add the spices and fry for 5 minutes over a low heat. If the mixture starts to burn, add 1 tablespoon of water. Stir in the ground beef and cook over a high heat until very well browned.
2 Meanwhile, bring a saucepan of water to the boil, add the potatoes and salt to taste. Lower the heat, cover, and cook gently for 5 minutes, then add the peas. Continue cooking until the potatoes and peas are tender. Drain the potatoes and peas and stir into the stew mixture until well combined. Serve hot.

Serves 4
Preparation time: 10 minutes
Cooking time: 30 minutes

Cook's Note
Garam masala is a dry spice mixture—*garam* means hot and *masala* means spices,—which varies from region to region. It may be added during cooking or used as a garnish. Many Indian cooks make up their own favorite blend of spices, but it is available ready-made from good supermarkets and Indian grocers.

Stuffed Eggplants

2 large eggplants
3 tablespoons vegetable oil
I onion, finely chopped
I garlic clove, finely chopped
2 green chilies, deseeded and finely
    chopped
I teaspoon turmeric
I lb. ground beef
I egg, lightly beaten
2–3 tablespoons fresh
    breadcrumbs
salt

Eggplants stuffed with ground beef and breadcrumbs and grilled.

1 Cook the whole eggplants in a large pan of salted boiling water for 15 minutes, or until almost tender. Drain thoroughly and leave to cool.
2 Heat the oil in a pan, add the onion, and fry until golden. Add the garlic, chilies, and turmeric and fry for 2 minutes. Add the ground beef and cook, stirring, until brown all over. Season with salt to taste and cook gently for 20 minutes, until the meat is tender.
3 Cut the eggplants in half lengthwise. Carefully scoop out the flesh. Add it to the meat mixture and mix well. Adjust the seasoning to taste. Fill the eggplant shells with the meat mixture, brush with the beaten egg, and cover with breadcrumbs. Place under a preheated moderate grill and cook for 4–5 minutes, until golden.

Serves 4
Preparation time: 15 minutes
Cooking time: 50 minutes

'"When food fails, the five senses fail."
Tamil Proverb

Beef Curry with Potatoes

1 Heat the oil in a large pan, add the onions and fry until lightly browned. Add the garlic, chili powder, cumin, ground coriander, and ginger and cook gently for 5 minutes, stirring occasionally. If the mixture becomes dry, add 2 tablespoons of water.

2 Add the cubes of beef and cook, stirring, until browned all over. Add the tomato paste, salt to taste and just enough water to cover the meat, then stir very well. Bring to the boil, cover and simmer for about 1 hour, or until the meat is almost tender. Add the potatoes and whole chilies and simmer until the potatoes are cooked.

Serves 4

Preparation time: 15 minutes
Cooking time: 1¼–1½ hours

4 tablespoons vegetable oil
2 onions, finely chopped
2 garlic cloves, chopped
1 teaspoon chili powder
1 tablespoon ground cumin
1½ tablespoons ground coriander
1 inch piece fresh ginger, finely chopped
1½ lb. stewing steak, cubed
2 tablespoons tomato paste
¾ lb. small new potatoes
4 green chilies
salt

Beef with Coconut Milk

3 tablespoons vegetable oil
2 onions, sliced
2 garlic cloves, finely chopped
3 green chilies, chopped
1½ inch piece fresh ginger, chopped
1½ lb. braising steak, cubed
½ teaspoon chili powder
1 teaspoon turmeric
1 teaspoon pepper
1 teaspoon ground cumin
½ teaspoon cinnamon
½ teaspoon ground cloves
1 cup coconut milk
½ cup vinegar
salt
2 yellow or green chilies, diced,
    to garnish

Cubed braising steak is cooked slowly with a subtle combination of spices and coconut milk, until the meat is tender and succulent and the sauce is rich and thick.

1 Heat the oil in a large pan, add the onions and fry until they are just beginning to brown, then add the garlic, chilies, and ginger. Fry for 1 minute, then add the beef and remaining spices. Stir well and cook for 5 minutes, stirring occasionally.
2 Add the coconut milk, which should just cover the meat; if it does not, add a little water. Add salt to taste. Bring to simmering point, cover and cook for about 1½ hours, until the meat is almost tender.
3 Add the vinegar and continue cooking for about 30 minutes, until the meat is tender and the gravy is thick. Serve garnished with diced chilies.

Serves 4
Preparation time: 20 minutes
Cooking time: 2–2¼ hours

Cook's Note
Instead of coconut milk in this recipe you could use 3 oz. creamed coconut, melted in 1 cup warm water. Creamed coconut is sold in blocks, which should always be softened in warm water before use.

Lamb Kebab

1¼ cup plain yogurt
1 tablespoon ground coriander
½ teaspoon chili powder
1 tablespoon vegetable oil
1½ lb. boned leg of lamb, cubed
4 onions
8 tomatoes
2 red peppers, cored, deseeded
    and cut into squares
salt
2 tablespoons finely chopped
    cilantro, to garnish

1 Put the yogurt, ground coriander, chili powder, oil, and salt to taste in a large bowl and stir to combine. Add the lamb, mix well, cover and leave in the refrigerator overnight.

2 Cut the onions into quarters and separate the layers. Cut the tomatoes in half.

3 Thread the pieces of onion, lamb and red pepper alternately on to 8 metal or presoaked wooden skewers, beginning and ending each kebab with a tomato half. Place under a preheated hot grill and cook for about 10 minutes, turning frequently and basting with any remaining marinade as necessary. Sprinkle with the chopped cilantro before serving.

Serves 4
Preparation time: 15 minutes, plus marinating
Cooking time: 10 minutes

"Hunger cannot be satisfied by eating froth."
Tamil proverb

Pork Vindaloo

This hot curry owes some of its kick to the combination of spices, including mustard seeds, and the addition of vinegar.

1 Mix the spices and a little salt with the vinegar. Put the onion, garlic, and pork into a bowl. Pour over the vinegar mixture, cover and leave in the refrigerator overnight.
2 Heat the oil in a large pan, add the pork mixture and bring to simmering point. Cover and cook for about 45 minutes, or until the pork is tender.

Serves 4
Preparation time: 10 minutes, plus marinating
Cooking time: 50 minutes

1–2 teaspoons chili powder
1 teaspoon turmeric
2 teaspoons ground cumin
2 teaspoons ground mustard seeds
2 tablespoons ground coriander
1½ inch piece fresh ginger, finely
    chopped
½ cup vinegar
1 large onion, finely chopped
2 garlic cloves, crushed
1½ lb. pork fillet, cubed
4 tablespoons vegetable oil
salt

Spiced Roast Lamb

5 lb. leg of lamb, skin and fat
  removed
2 in. piece fresh ginger, chopped
6 garlic cloves
grated rind of 1 lemon
8 tablespoons lemon juice
2 teaspoons cumin seeds
6 cardamom pods, peeled
1 teaspoon ground cloves
1 teaspoon turmeric
1½ teaspoons chili powder
1 tablespoon salt
1¼ cup plain yogurt
1 cup whole unpeeled almonds
4 tablespoons brown sugar
1 teaspoon saffron threads, infused
  in 3 tablespoons boiling water
Saffron Rice, to serve
  (see page 114)

A leg of lamb that is coated in a mixture of spices and cooked slowly to allow the flavors to fully develop.

1 Prick the lamb all over with a fork and make about 12 deep cuts in the meat.
2 Blend the ginger, garlic, lemon rind and juice, spices, and salt in a blender or food processor. Spread the paste over the lamb and leave to stand for 1 hour in a flameproof casserole.
3 Blend 4 tablespoons of the plain yogurt with the almonds and 2 tablespoons of the sugar in a blender or food processor. Stir in the remaining yogurt and pour over the lamb. Cover the casserole tightly and leave for 48 hours in the refrigerator.
4 Let the meat return to room temperature. Sprinkle over the remaining sugar and cook, uncovered, in a preheated oven, 425°F, for 30 minutes. Cover, reduce the temperature to 325°F, and cook for 3 hours, basting occasionally. Sprinkle the saffron water over the meat and cook for a further 30 minutes, or until very tender.
5 Remove the meat from the casserole, wrap it in foil, and keep warm. Skim off the fat from the liquid in the casserole and boil the sauce until thick. Place the meat on a warmed dish and pour over the sauce. Carve into thick slices and serve with Saffron Rice.

Serves 6
Preparation time: 20 minutes, plus standing and marinating
Cooking time: 4 hours
Oven temperature: 425°F, then 325°F

Dry Pork Curry

1½ lb. pork tenderloin
2 tablespoons coriander seeds,
    roughly pounded with a pestle
    and mortar
1 teaspoon pepper
1 tablespoon paprika
4 tablespoons vegetable oil
salt
2 tablespoons finely chopped
    cilantro, to garnish (optional)
tomato and red onion salad,
    to serve

1 Slit the pork fillets lengthwise and cut each half into quarters. Prick the pieces all over with a fork. Mix together the coriander seeds, pepper, paprika, and salt to taste and rub into the meat on both sides. Leave to stand for 1 hour.

2 Heat the oil in a pan, add the meat and fry quickly on both sides to seal. Reduce the heat and sauté for 5 minutes or until cooked through, stirring and turning to prevent burning.

3 Sprinkle with the cilantro and serve with a tomato and red onion salad.

Serves 4
Preparation time: 10–15 minutes, plus standing
Cooking time: 10 minutes

Lamb with Almonds

This is a delicious combination of cubed lamb gently cooked in mildly spiced yogurt with flaked almonds.

1 Heat 2 tablespoons of the oil in a pan, add 1 chopped onion and fry until golden. Add the lamb and 6 oz. of the yogurt. Stir well, cover and simmer for 20 minutes.
2 Place the garlic, ginger, green chilies, coriander seeds, cumin seeds, mint, cilantro, and 2–3 tablespoons yogurt in a blender or food processor and blend to a paste.
3 Heat the remaining oil in a large pan, add the cardamoms, cloves and cinnamon stick and fry for 1 minute, stirring. Add the second chopped onion and the prepared paste and fry for 5 minutes, stirring constantly.
4 Add the lamb and yogurt mixture, add salt to taste, stir well and bring to simmering point. Cover and cook for 30 minutes. Add the almonds and cook for a further 15 minutes, until the meat is tender. Serve garnished with flaked almonds.

Serves 4
Preparation time: 10–15 minutes
Cooking time: 1¼ hours

4 tablespoons vegetable oil
2 onions, finely chopped
1½ lb. boned leg of lamb, cubed
1¼ cup plain yogurt
2 garlic cloves
1 inch piece fresh ginger
2 green chilies
1 tablespoon coriander seeds
1 teaspoon cumin seeds
1 teaspoon chopped fresh mint leaves
1 teaspoon chopped cilantro
6 cardamom pods
6 cloves
1 inch piece cinnamon stick
1 cup flaked almonds, plus extra to garnish
salt

"A full belly makes a heavy head."
Bihan proverb

Lamb Korma

1½ lb. boneless leg of lamb, cubed
⅓ cup plain yogurt
½ teaspoon saffron threads, infused
   in 2 tablespoons boiling water
   for 10 minutes
1 teaspoon salt
2 tablespoons ghee
¼ teaspoon ground cardamom
½ teaspoon cinnamon
1½ teaspoons ground cumin
1½ teaspoons ground coriander
1 cup coconut milk
2 tablespoons chopped cilantro
½ teaspoon sugar

BLENDED MIXTURE:
2 onions, chopped
3 garlic cloves, chopped
1 inch piece fresh ginger, chopped
2 green chilies, deseeded and
   chopped
½ cup ground almonds
½ cup water

TO GARNISH:
cilantro leaves
¼ cup flaked almonds, toasted

A favorite mild lamb curry cooked with yogurt, coconut milk, saffron, and ground almonds.

1 Place the pieces of lamb in a bowl. Mix together the yogurt, saffron and its water and the salt. Pour over the lamb, cover and leave to marinate for 2 hours.
2 Place the ingredients for the blended mixture in a blender or food processor and blend to a thick paste. Set aside.
3 Heat the ghee in a pan, add the ground cardamom, cinnamon, cumin, and ground coriander and cook over a gentle heat for 1 minute. Stir in the blended paste and cook, stirring frequently, for a further 5 minutes.
4 Add the coconut milk and the lamb and saffron yogurt, bring to the boil, then lower the heat. Cover the pan and cook very gently, stirring occasionally, for 45 minutes, or until the lamb is tender and the sauce is thick.
5 Stir in the chopped cilantro and the sugar and serve hot, garnished with cilantro leaves and toasted flaked almonds.

Serves 4–6
Preparation time: 25 minutes, plus marinating
Cooking time: 1 hour

Cook's Note
Ghee is a type of clarified butter, which is made by heating ordinary butter to remove the milk solids. It has a higher burning point than most other oils and is therefore ideal for frying delicate foods. Vegetable ghee is readily available and is a healthier alternative to standard ghee, with a slightly different flavor and texture. Vegetable oil is an acceptable substitute.

Kashmiri Kofta Curry

A fragrant meatball curry that goes well with Indian bread such as Naan (see page 122).

1 To make the lamb meatballs, place the lamb, ginger, red chili, cilantro, 1 teaspoon of the garam masala, 1 teaspoon of the salt, and the pepper in a bowl. Mix thoroughly, then divide the mixture into 16 and shape each portion into a small meatball.
2 Heat the oil in a heavy-based frying pan, add the meatballs, and fry over a gentle heat for 5 minutes, turning occasionally to seal them. Using a slotted spoon, transfer the meatballs to a saucepan.
3 In a jar, mix together the yogurt, sugar, chili powder, the remaining garam masala, and salt and the water. Pour the yogurt mixture over the meatballs, then cook the curry, uncovered, over a medium heat for 10 minutes, or until the meatballs are cooked and most of the liquid has been absorbed, leaving just a little sauce.
4 Serve hot, garnished with ground cardamom and cilantro sprigs.

Serves 4
Preparation time: 20 minutes
Cooking time: 20 minutes

1 lb. lean ground lamb
1 tablespoon grated fresh ginger
1 large red chili, deseeded and
    very finely chopped
2 tablespoons chopped cilantro
1 tablespoon garam masala
1½ teaspoons salt
¼ teaspoon pepper
3 tablespoons vegetable oil
⅓ cup plain yogurt
1 teaspoon soft brown sugar
½ teaspoon chili powder
1 cup water

TO GARNISH:
pinch of ground cardamom
sprigs of cilantro

Goan Lamb and Pork Curry

3 tablespoons vegetable oil
2 onions, finely chopped
3 garlic cloves, crushed
1 tablespoon grated fresh ginger
2 large red chilies, quartered
    lengthwise and deseeded
¾ lb. lamb tenderloin, cut into bite-
    sized pieces
¾ lb. lean pork, cut into bite-sized
    pieces
1 teaspoon salt
½ cup water
½ cup distilled malt vinegar
1 green and 1 red chili, cut into
    rings, to garnish
Saffron Rice, to serve
    (see page 114)

SPICE MIXTURE:
1 teaspoon ground cumin
1 teaspoon ground coriander
1 teaspoon chili powder
1 tablespoon black mustard seeds
1 tablespoon black onion seeds
    (kalonji)
1 tablespoon garam masala

An unusual curry from Goa in which two types of meat are cooked together.

1 Heat the oil in a heavy-based pan, add the onions, garlic, ginger, and chilies and cook over a low heat, stirring frequently, for about 5 minutes, until softened.
2 Place the ingredients for the spice mixture in an electric spice mill or use a pestle and mortar and grind to produce a fine powder. Add the ground spices to the pan and fry for a further 1 minute.
3 Add the pieces of lamb and pork to the pan, together with the salt. Coat the meat in the spices and cook for 2 minutes. Add the water and the vinegar to the pan and stir well to combine the ingredients. Cover and simmer over a gentle heat, stirring occasionally, for about 45 minutes, or until the meat is tender.
4 Remove the lid, increase the heat and cook for another 15 minutes, stirring frequently, until the sauce is thick and dark. Taste and adjust the seasoning if necessary.
5 Transfer the curry to a warmed serving dish and garnish with chili rings. Serve with Saffron Rice.

Serves 6
Preparation time: 15–20 minutes
Cooking time: 1¼ hours

Lamb Tikka Masala

1½ lb. lean lamb, cubed
1 quantity Tandoori Marinade
   (see page 56)

MASALA SAUCE:
4 tablespoons ghee
1 quantity Curry Purée
   (see page 48)
1 tablespoon tandoori paste
2 teaspoons tomato paste
2 tomatoes, skinned and chopped
1 red pepper, cored, deseeded and
   puréed
1 tablespoon chopped cilantro
1 tablespoon ground almonds
2 tablespoons single cream
white sugar, to taste
salt

TO GARNISH:
lime slices, quartered
sprigs of parsley

Cubes of lamb are marinated in a tandoori marinade, then cooked on skewers and added to a masala sauce.

1 Combine the lamb and tandoori marinade in a bowl. Cover and leave in the refrigerator for about 24 hours.
2 Remove the pieces of lamb from the marinade, reserving the marinade. Thread the pieces of lamb onto 4 metal or presoaked wooden skewers and and cook under a preheated moderate grill for 15–20 minutes, turning them once halfway through the cooking time.
3 Meanwhile, make the masala sauce. Heat the ghee in a large frying pan or wok. Stir-fry the curry purée for 5 minutes. Add the tandoori paste and the reserved marinade and stir-fry for 2 minutes. Add the tomato paste, chopped tomatoes, and puréed red pepper. Bring to simmering point and add a little water, if necessary, to achieve a creamy textured sauce. Add the cilantro, ground almonds, cream, and sugar and salt to taste.
4 When the lamb tikkas are cooked, remove them from the skewers and stir them into the masala sauce. Serve garnished with lime slices and parsley.

Serves 4
Preparation time: 30 minutes, plus marinating
Cooking time: 25–30 minutes

Spicy Beef Curry

Marinated beef cooked with milk, almonds, and coconut.

1 Slice the beef into 4 steaks. Beat with a rolling pin or the back of a wooden spoon until they are ¼ inch thick. Cut each steak in half to give 8 pieces. Place the steaks in a nonmetallic dish. Add the red wine and spices and leave to marinate in the refrigerator for up to 24 hours.

2 Heat the oil in a frying pan or wok and stir-fry the curry purée for 5 minutes. Add the curry paste and mix well. Lift the steaks out of the marinade and add to the pan 2 at a time. Fry the steaks quickly to seal—allowing about 20 seconds on each side. When all the steaks are in the pan and are brown, add the milk, ground almonds, coconut, and the marinade. Simmer for 10 minutes, until the meat is cooked.

3 Transfer to a warmed serving dish and pour the cream over the top. Garnish with parsley and pistachio nuts and serve with rice.

Serves 4
Preparation time: 20 minutes, plus marinating
Cooking time: 15–20 minutes

Cook's Note
Curry pastes are available in different strengths and flavors. A curry paste is simply a "wet" blend of spices—as opposed to a "dry" blend such as garam masala—cooked with oil and vinegar, which help to preserve them.

1½ lb. lean beef rump roast
½ cup red wine
4 tablespoons vegetable oil
1 quantity Curry Purée
  (see page 48)
1 tablespoon mild curry paste
¾ cup milk
2 tablespoons ground almonds
2 tablespoons dried coconut
  (unsweetened)
4 tablespoons heavy cream
salt

SPICES:
2 teaspoons garam masala
1 teaspoon mace
½ teaspoon cinnamon

TO GARNISH:
sprigs of parsley
chopped pistachio nuts
steamed or boiled rice, to serve

Lamb and Vegetable Curry

½ cup lentils
½ cup chickpeas
½ cup yellow mung (moong dhal)
1½ lb. lamb loin, cut into
    2 inch cubes
3 tablespoons ghee
I large onion, thinly sliced
2 tablespoons tomato paste
I cup water
salt and pepper

VEGETABLES:
I small eggplant, cubed
I small winter squash, peeled and
    cubed
I medium-small potato, peeled and
    cubed
2 onions, roughly chopped
2 tomatoes, skinned and chopped
2 handfuls fresh spinach, washed

MASALA MIXTURE:
3 red chilies, deseeded and
    chopped
3 green chilies, deseeded and
    chopped
6 garlic cloves, crushed
I inch piece fresh ginger, finely
    chopped
¼ cup cilantro leaves
I tablespoon mint leaves
4 tablespoons water

DRY SPICE MIXTURE:
2 teaspoons turmeric
I teaspoon black mustard seeds
½ teaspoon cinnamon
¼ teaspoon fenugreek powder
2 tablespoons dhana jeera powder
4 cardamom pods, crushed

TO GARNISH:
sprigs of cilantro
deep-fried onion rings
red chilies, cut into rings
boiled rice or Saffron Rice,
    to serve (see page 114)

A spicy curry that is cooked with lentils in masala and a dry spice mixture.

1 The night before, wash the lentils, chickpeas, and moong dhal in several changes of cold water and leave them to soak overnight in a large bowl of cold water.

2 The next day, drain the pulses and place them in a large pan with the cubed lamb. Pour over enough boiling water to cover and season generously with salt. Bring to the boil, skim any fat from the surface, then cover and simmer the pulses and meat, stirring occasionally, for about 20 minutes.

3 Add all the prepared vegetables to the pan, stir well and continue cooking for a further 40 minutes, until the pulses and vegetables are cooked and the lamb is tender. Drain the liquid from the pan and remove the pieces of meat using a slotted spoon. Set the meat aside and tip the cooked vegetables and pulses into a blender or food processor. Blend to produce a thick purée. Pour into a bowl and set aside.

4 Heat the ghee in a large, heavy-based frying pan and fry the thinly sliced onion over a gentle heat for 5 minutes, until softened and golden.

5 Place all the ingredients for the masala mixture in the blender or food processor and blend to a paste. Add this paste to the softened onion in the frying pan and cook over a low heat for a further 3 minutes. Stir in the dry spice mixture and cook, stirring constantly, for 3 minutes, until the mixture is aromatic.

6 Add the pieces of lamb and the pulse and vegetable purée to the pan, together with the tomato paste and water. Season with salt and pepper, cover and simmer the curry for about 30 minutes until it is thick. If it becomes too dry during cooking, add a little more water to the pan. Taste and adjust the seasoning if necessary.

7 Transfer the curry to a warmed serving dish. Garnish with cilantro sprigs, deep-fried onion rings and chili rings and serve immediately with boiled rice or Saffron Rice.

Serves 6
Preparation time: 40 minutes, plus soaking
Cooking time: 1¼ hours

Beef with Fenugreek

4 tablespoons ghee
2 tablespoons mild curry paste
1½ lb. stewing beef, cubed
4 tomatoes, chopped
4 tablespoons dried fenugreek
   leaves (methi)
1 tablespoon garam masala
salt
2 tablespoons chopped parsley,
   to garnish

CURRY PURÉE:
6 tablespoons ghee
2–4 garlic cloves, finely chopped
2 inch piece fresh ginger, finely
   chopped
½ onion, finely chopped
2 teaspoons mild curry paste
1 teaspoon tomato paste
1 tablespoon chopped cilantro

Cubes of beef cooked with dried fenugreek leaves produce this moist savory curry.

1 To make the curry purée, heat the ghee in a large frying pan or wok. Stir-fry the garlic for 1 minute. Add the ginger and stir-fry for 1 more minute. Add the onion and stir-fry for 2–3 minutes more. Stir in the curry paste, tomato paste, and cilantro with enough water to prevent the mixture from sticking. Simmer for 5 minutes.
2 Heat the ghee in another large frying pan or wok and stir-fry the curry purée for 5 minutes. Stir the curry paste well to blend and add the cubes of beef. Stir-fry for about 5 minutes more to seal the meat.
3 Transfer the meat and sauce to a heavy lidded casserole and bake in a preheated oven, 375°F, for 20 minutes. Stir in the tomatoes, dried fenugreek, garam masala, and salt to taste, with a little water to moisten if necessary. Continue cooking for another 25 minutes.
If at the end of the cooking time there is an excess of oil, skim it off before serving. Garnish with chopped parsley.

Serves 4
Preparation time: 15 minutes
Cooking time: 1 hour 10 minutes
Oven temperature: 375°F

Cook's Note
Fenugreek leaves, called *methi*, are widely used, fresh or dried, in Indian cooking. The plant is rich in protein, minerals, and vitamins, which makes it an important ingredient in vegetable and dhal dishes eaten in the poorer areas of India.

"What's in the pot will be what's in the spoon."

Tamil proverb

Beef and Mango Curry

This Nepalese recipe combines stewing beef with a pickle base and fresh mango.

1 Heat the ghee in a large frying pan or wok and stir-fry the curry purée for 5 minutes. Stir in the curry paste and the meat, combining the ingredients well. Continue frying until the meat is sealed—about 5 minutes.

2 Transfer to a heavy lidded casserole and place in a preheated oven, 375°F, for 20 minutes.

3 Meanwhile, scoop all the flesh from the mango. Place it in a blender or food processor and work to a purée. Add it to the casserole with the chopped pickle, cilantro, and salt to taste, with a little water to moisten if necessary.

4 Return the casserole to the oven for a further 25 minutes. At the end of the cooking time, spoon off any excess oil before serving. Garnish with fresh mango slices and sprigs of parsley.

Serves 4
Preparation time: 10 minutes
Cooking time: 55 minutes
Oven temperature: 375°F

4 tablespoons ghee
1 quantity Curry Purée
   (see page 48)
1 tablespoon mild curry paste
1½ lb. stewing beef, cubed
1 fresh mango
3 tablespoons mild mango or
   brinjal pickle, finely chopped
1 tablespoon chopped cilantro
salt

TO GARNISH:
fresh mango slices
sprigs of parsley

Goan Vindaloo

1½ lb. pork tenderloin, cubed
1 scant cup vinegar
2–6 teaspoons chili powder
4 tablespoons ghee
1 quantity Curry Purée
   (see page 48)
4–8 fresh or dried red chilies
salt
sprigs of basil, to garnish

SPICES:
(DRY-ROASTED AND GROUND)
2 teaspoons coriander seeds
1 teaspoon white cumin seeds
4 inch piece cinnamon stick
12 cloves
12 green cardamom pods
2 teaspoons black pepper

A hot pork curry cooked with dry-roasted spices, chili powder, and chilies.

1 Place the pork in a nonmetallic dish with the vinegar and a quantity of chili powder according to your taste. Cover and refrigerate for 24 hours.
2 Mix the dry-roasted and ground spices with enough water to make a paste. Heat the ghee in a large frying pan or wok and stir-fry the curry purée for 5 minutes. Add the spice paste, stir-frying for 2 minutes more. Lift the pieces of pork out of the marinade, reserving the liquid, and combine them with the ingredients in the frying pan.
3 Transfer the mixture to a heavy-lidded casserole and bake in a preheated oven, 375°F, for 1 hour, adding the red chilies to taste after 20 minutes of cooking time, with a little salt and some marinade to moisten if necessary. If at the end of the cooking time there is an excess of oil, spoon it off before serving. Garnish with sprigs of basil.

Serves 4
Preparation time: 15 minutes, plus marinating
Cooking time: 1½ hours
Oven temperature: 375°F

Cook's Note
Dry-roasting spices brings out a more intense flavor. Place them whole in a heavy-based dry frying pan and shake the pan over a fairly high heat for 1–2 minutes. Cool slightly, then grind the dry-roasted spices to a powder using an electric spice mill or a mortar and pestle.

Lamb with Yogurt

Cubed lamb, cooked with yogurt, ginger, and dry-roasted cumin seeds.

1 Melt the ghee in a heavy-based frying pan or wok and fry half the onions over a very low heat, until soft and golden brown. Remove from the pan with a slotted spoon and set aside.
2 Increase the heat, add the meat and sauté until it is sealed on all sides. Remove the meat from the pan and set aside.
3 Add the chili powder, ginger, salt, and the remaining onions to the pan, then stir in the yogurt. Cook for 2 minutes, then return the meat to the pan. Cover and simmer for 10 minutes.
4 Add the garlic, cardamom seeds, garam masala, ground cumin seeds, and the browned onions. Cover and simmer for 30 minutes, or until the lamb is tender, adding a little water if necessary to prevent it from sticking to the bottom of the wok. Serve hot.

Serves 4
Preparation time: 15–20 minutes
Cooking time: 50 minutes

¼ cup ghee
1 lb. onions, sliced
1 lb. boned shoulder of lamb, cut into 1 inch cubes
1 teaspoon chili powder
½ teaspoon ground ginger
1 teaspoon salt
1¼ cup plain yogurt
2 garlic cloves, crushed
4 cardamom seeds
1 teaspoon garam masala
½ teaspoon cumin seeds, dry-roasted and ground (see page 50)

Balti Beef *pictured*

4 tablespoons vegetable oil
1 large onion, chopped
½ teaspoon ground coriander
½ teaspoon turmeric
1 inch piece fresh ginger, finely
    chopped
1 garlic clove, crushed
1 red chili, chopped
1 yellow chili, chopped
1 lb. frying steak, cut into strips
    about 1 x 1¾ inches
1 green or red pepper, cored,
    deseeded and roughly chopped
2 tomatoes, quartered
4 tablespoons lemon juice
salt
cilantro leaves, to garnish

1 Heat the oil in a heavy-based frying pan or wok, add the onion and fry until soft. Add the ground coriander, turmeric, ginger, garlic, and chili and stir-fry over a low heat for 5 minutes. If the mixture becomes dry, add 1 tablespoon of water.
2 Add the steak, increase the heat and stir-fry until browned all over. Add the chopped pepper, then cover and cook over a low heat for 5–10 minutes, stirring occasionally, until the meat is tender. Add the tomatoes, lemon juice, and salt to taste and cook, uncovered, for 2–3 minutes. Serve hot.

Serves 2–3
Preparation time: 20 minutes
Cooking time: 25 minutes

Calcutta Beef Curry

1 teaspoon salt
1 tablespoon chili powder
2 teaspoons ground coriander
1 teaspoon pepper
1½ teaspoons turmeric
1 teaspoon ground cumin
3½ cups milk
2–2½ lb. braising steak, trimmed
    and cut into 1¾ inch cubes
2 tablespoons ghee
2 large onions, thinly sliced
5 garlic cloves, thinly sliced
3 inch piece fresh ginger, peeled
    and thinly sliced
2 teaspoons garam masala

This rich and hearty curry consists of beef simmered for a long time in a mixture of milk and spices until the meat is tender and the sauce reduced.

1 Put the salt, chili powder, ground coriander, pepper, turmeric, and cumin into a large bowl. Mix in a little of the milk to make a paste, then gradually stir in the remaining milk. Add the cubes of beef and stir well until the beef is evenly coated.
2 Melt the ghee in a heavy-based frying pan or wok, add the onions, garlic and ginger and fry gently for 4–5 minutes, until soft.
3 Remove the beef from the milk and spice mixture with a slotted spoon, add to the pan and stir-fry over a moderate heat until browned on all sides.
4 Increase the heat, add the milk and spice mixture and bring to the boil. Cover the pan, lower the heat and cook gently for 1½–2 hours, or until the beef is tender and the sauce reduced.
5 Just before serving, sprinkle in the garam masala. Increase the heat and boil off any excess liquid to leave a thick sauce. Transfer to a warmed serving dish and serve immediately.

Serves 4–6
Preparation time: 15 minutes
Cooking time: about 2 hours

chicken

In Indian cooking, the skin of the chicken is almost always removed before cooking. This allows the flavor of the spices to penetrate the chicken much better, as well as making the entire dish less fatty. Chicken is often marinated and grilled—as in chicken tikka and chicken tandoori—or stewed with spices. There are also innumerable chicken curry dishes.

Chicken Tikka Masala

1½ lb. skinless, boneless chicken
   breasts, cubed
9–12 tablespoons fresh lemon juice
   or 6 tablespoons bottled
   lemon juice
1 quantity Tandoori Marinade
   (see below)

TANDOORI MARINADE:
⅓ cup plain yogurt
⅓ cup + 1 tablespoon milk
2 tablespoons tandoori masala
1 tablespoon mild curry powder
   or paste
2 teaspoons garam masala
½–4 teaspoons chili powder
1 tablespoon chopped mint
1 tablespoon chopped cilantro
2 teaspoons garlic purée
1 inch piece fresh ginger, finely
   chopped
1 teaspoon white cumin seeds,
   dry-roasted and ground
   (see page 50)
2 tablespoons lemon juice

MASALA SAUCE:
4 tablespoons ghee
1 quantity Curry Purée
   (see page 48)
1 tablespoon tandoori paste
2 teaspoons tomato paste
2 tomatoes, skinned and chopped
1 red pepper, cored, deseeded, and
   puréed
1 tablespoon chopped cilantro
1 tablespoon ground almonds
2 tablespoons single cream
white sugar, to taste
salt

TO GARNISH:
diced tomato
sprigs of cilantro, chopped

1 Place the chicken in a large bowl and add the lemon juice, working it in with your fingers to "degrease" the chicken in preparation for the marinade. Leave to stand for 1 hour.
2 Combine the ingredients for the tandoori marinade in another large bowl, setting aside 2 tablespoons of the marinade to use later. Strain off and discard the juices from the chicken, then add the chicken to the marinade and stir well. Cover and refrigerate for a minimum of 6 hours, or overnight, but preferably for 24 hours.
3 Remove the pieces of chicken from the marinade and thread onto metal or presoaked wooden skewers and place them under a preheated moderate grill for 10–15 minutes, turning them 2 or 3 times. (Alternatively, the tikkas can be baked in a preheated oven, 375°F, or stir-fried, without oil, for about 15 minutes.)
4 Meanwhile, make the masala sauce. Heat the ghee in a large frying pan or wok. Stir-fry the curry purée for 5 minutes. Add the tandoori paste and reserved marinade and stir-fry for 2 minutes. Add the tomato paste, tomatoes, and puréed red pepper. Bring to simmering point and add a little water if necessary, to achieve a creamy textured sauce. Add the cilantro, ground almonds, cream, and sugar and salt to taste.
5 When the tikkas are cooked, remove them from the skewers, if using, and stir them into the sauce. Garnish with diced tomato and chopped cilantro.

Serves 4
Preparation time: 30 minutes, plus standing and marinating
Cooking time: 20–25 minutes

Chicken Korma

2 onions
2 garlic cloves
1 inch piece fresh ginger, chopped
2 green chilies, chopped
1 tablespoon coriander seeds
1 teaspoon salt
2 tablespoons water
½ cup almonds
1½ lb. chicken pieces, skinned
3 tablespoons vegetable oil
6 cardamom pods
6 cloves
1 inch piece cinnamon stick
⅔ cup plain yogurt
½ cup cream
¼ teaspoon powdered saffron,
    infused in 1 tablespoon warm
    water
2 tablespoons chopped cilantro, to
    garnish

1 Chop 1 onion and place in a blender or food processor with the garlic, ginger, chilies, coriander seeds, salt, water, and half the almonds. Blend until smooth. Place the pieces of chicken in a nonmetallic dish. Spoon the mixture over them, mix well, and set aside for 1 hour.
2 Finely chop the second onion. Heat the oil in a pan, add the onion, cardamoms, cloves, and cinnamon and fry until the onion is soft. Add the chicken and marinade and fry, stirring, until dry.
3 Add the yogurt, a tablespoon at a time, stirring until absorbed. Cover the pan and leave to simmer very gently for 30 minutes, adding a little water if necessary.
4 Place the remaining almonds, the cream, and saffron with its infused water in the blender or food processor and blend until smooth. Stir into the chicken and check the seasoning. Cover and simmer for about 5 more minutes, until the chicken is tender.
5 Serve garnished with chopped cilantro.

Serves 4
Preparation time: 15 minutes, plus marinating
Cooking time: 45–50 minutes

"Sing his praise, who gives you food."

Bihan proverb

Chicken Jalfrezi

1 Heat the ghee in a large frying pan or wok. Stir-fry the cumin and mustard seeds for 1 minute. Add the garlic and stir-fry for 1 minute more. Add the ginger and stir-fry for 2 minutes. Add the sliced onion and stir-fry until golden—about 5 minutes.

2 Combine the chicken pieces with the ingredients in the pan, stirring and turning for 5 more minutes. Add all the remaining ingredients and stir-fry for about 10 more minutes. Serve immediately.

Serves 4

Preparation time: 20 minutes
Cooking time: 25 minutes

Cook's Note

Chili Chicken: For a much hotter version, prepare as above but add 2–10 chopped green chilies instead of the peppers—the quantity of chilies depends on your heat threshold!

6 tablespoons ghee
1 teaspoon white cumin seeds
1 teaspoon black mustard seeds
2–6 garlic cloves, finely chopped
2 inch piece fresh ginger, finely sliced
1 large onion, thinly sliced
1½ lb. skinless, boneless chicken breasts, cubed
1 tablespoon mild curry paste
½ red pepper, cored, deseeded, and chopped
½ green pepper, cored, deseeded, and chopped
1 tablespoon chopped cilantro leaves
1–2 tablespoons water

Chicken Makhani

1½ lb. skinless, boneless chicken breasts or thighs, cut into 2 inch pieces
3 tablespoons vegetable oil

MARINADE:
3 large red chilies, deseeded, and chopped
4 garlic cloves, crushed
2 teaspoons dry-roasted cumin seeds, crushed
1 teaspoon garam masala
½ teaspoon salt
2 tablespoons cilantro leaves
4 tablespoons lemon juice
⅔ cup plain yogurt

SAUCE:
3 lb. ripe tomatoes, quartered
¼ cup butter
½ cup heavy cream
salt

TO GARNISH:
sprigs of cilantro
red chili, diced
Naan bread, to serve
    (see page 122)

Tomatoes and butter are the characteristic ingredients of a makhani, a refined and elegant dish.

1 Start by making the marinade. Place the chilies, garlic, and cumin seeds in a blender or food processor and blend briefly. Add the remaining marinade ingredients and work to a paste.
2 Transfer the marinade to a nonmetallic bowl. Add the chicken pieces to the marinade, turning to coat them evenly. Cover and refrigerate for 3 hours.
3 Meanwhile, prepare the sauce. Place the tomatoes in a large pan and cook them gently, with no added water, for about 20 minutes or until they are tender. Rub them through a fine sieve into a clean pan. Simmer the tomato pulp, stirring occasionally, for 30–40 minutes, until it is thick and reduced.
4 Stir in the butter and some salt and cook the sauce over a medium heat, stirring often, for a further 30 minutes, until it is thick. Stir in the cream and heat it through. Taste and adjust the amount of salt if necessary and set the sauce aside.
5 Heat the oil in a large heavy-based frying pan. Remove the chicken pieces from their marinade, reserving the marinade, and fry them gently to seal, for about 5 minutes. Add the marinade to the pan, increase the heat and cook, stirring frequently, for a further 12 minutes, or until the chicken is cooked through.
6 Reduce the heat and pour the tomato sauce over the chicken. Simmer gently for a further 5 minutes.
7 Transfer the chicken to a warmed serving dish and garnish with cilantro leaves and diced chili. Serve with Naan bread.

Serves 4
Preparation time: 30 minutes, plus marinating
Cooking time: 2 hours

Kashmiri Chicken

½ cup butter
3 large onions, finely sliced
10 peppercorns
1 cardamom pod
2 inch piece cinnamon stick
2 inch piece fresh ginger, chopped
2 garlic cloves, finely chopped
1 teaspoon chili powder
2 teaspoons paprika
3 lb. chicken pieces, skinned
1 cup plain yogurt
salt

The addition of plain yogurt toward the end of the cooking time gives this dish a deliciously mild and creamy flavor, which makes a wonderful contrast to all the spices.

1 Melt the butter in a deep, lidded frying pan. Add the onions, peppercorns, cardamom, and cinnamon and fry until the onions are golden. Add the ginger, garlic, chili powder, paprika, and salt to taste and fry for 2 minutes, stirring occasionally.
2 Add the chicken pieces and fry until browned. Gradually add the yogurt, stirring constantly. Cover and cook gently for about 30 minutes. Serve hot.

Serves 6
Preparation time: 10 minutes
Cooking time: 40–45 minutes

Chicken Curry

1 Place the garlic, ginger, turmeric, cumin, chili powder, pepper, cilantro, yogurt, and salt to taste in a large bowl. Mix well, add the chicken pieces and leave for 4 hours, turning occasionally.
2 Heat the oil in a pan, add the onions and fry until golden. Add the chicken and the marinade. Bring to simmering point, cover and cook for about 30 minutes, until the chicken is tender.

Serves 4

Preparation time: 5–10 minutes, plus marinating
Cooking time: 40 minutes

2 garlic cloves, chopped
2 inch piece fresh ginger, chopped
1 teaspoon turmeric
2 teaspoons cumin seeds, ground
1 teaspoon chili powder
1 teaspoon pepper
3 tablespoons finely chopped
   cilantro
2 cups plain yogurt
2 lb. chicken pieces, skinned
4 tablespoons vegetable oil
2 onions, chopped
salt

"A pot cooks best on its own stove."

Hindi proverb

Chicken with Spinach

3 tablespoons vegetable oil
2 onions, chopped
2 garlic cloves, crushed
1 inch piece fresh ginger, chopped
2 teaspoons ground coriander
1 teaspoon chili powder
1½ lb. chicken legs and thighs,
  skinned
1½ lb. spinach
2–3 tablespoons milk, to mix
  (optional)
salt

1 Heat the oil in a large frying pan. Add the onions and fry until soft and golden. Add the garlic, ginger, ground coriander, chili powder, and season with salt to taste, then fry gently for 2 minutes, stirring constantly.

2 Add the chicken pieces and fry on all sides until browned. Add the spinach, stir well, cover and simmer for 35 minutes, until the chicken is tender.

3 If the mixture becomes too dry during cooking, stir in a little milk. If there is too much liquid left at the end of cooking, uncover the pan and cook for a few minutes more until the liquid has evaporated.

Serves 4
Preparation time: 10 minutes
Cooking time: 45–50 minutes

Chicken and Dhal Curry

1 cup red lentils (masoor dhal)
2 cups water
3 tablespoons vegetable oil
2 onions, finely chopped
2 garlic cloves, crushed
1 inch piece fresh ginger, finely chopped
1 tablespoon ground coriander
1 teaspoon ground cumin
½ teaspoon turmeric
½ teaspoon ground cloves
2 teaspoons chili powder
1½ lb. chicken thighs
salt

1 Wash the lentils in several changes of cold water, then leave to soak in a bowl of clean water for 1 hour. Drain the lentils and boil in the measured water with 1 teaspoon salt added, for about 1 hour, until soft. Drain and set aside.

2 Heat the oil in a pan, add the onions, garlic, and ginger and fry for about 5 minutes. Add the spices and salt to taste and fry gently for 10 minutes. If the mixture becomes too dry, add 2 tablespoons water. Add the chicken thighs and fry until golden all over. Add the cooked lentils, cover and simmer for about 30 minutes, or until the chicken is tender.

Serves 4
Preparation time: 10–15 minutes, plus standing
Cooking time: 1¾–2 hours

Cook's Note
Dhal are pulses or lentils and are widely used in Indian cooking. There are many different types and all are good sources of protein. Masoor dhal are widely available and are split, skinless lentils, known as red lentils, although they are actually pinky-orange in color. Recipes vary but, on the whole, lentils do not really need soaking before use. They should, however, be washed in several changes of cold water before being cooked.

Tandoori Chicken

1 Mix together the chili powder, pepper, salt, and lemon juice. Slash the chicken all over and rub the mixture into the cuts. Set aside for 1 hour.

2 Place the yogurt, garlic, ginger, chilies and coriander and cumin seeds in a blender or food processor and work to a paste. Spread it all over the chicken. Cover and leave in the refrigerator overnight. The next day return the chicken to room temperature before cooking.

3 Place the chicken on a rack in a roasting tin and pour over half the melted butter. Cook in a preheated oven, 400°F, for 1 hour, or until tender. Baste occasionally and pour over the remaining butter halfway through the cooking time.

Serves 4

Preparation time: 10 minutes, plus marinating
Cooking time: 1 hour
Oven temperature: 400°F

Cook's Notes

If preferred, the chicken can be spit-roasted for about 1 hour, using all the butter at the start. The typical red color of tandoori chicken comes from a food coloring, available at specialty Asian grocers. It has been omitted from this recipe because many people are allergic to it.

½–1 teaspoon chili powder
1 teaspoon pepper
1 teaspoon salt
2 tablespoons lemon juice
3 lb. oven-ready chicken, skinned
4 tablespoons plain yogurt
3 garlic cloves
2 inch piece fresh ginger
2 small dried red chilies
1 tablespoon coriander seeds
2 teaspoons cumin seeds
¼ cup butter, melted

Chicken Stuffed with Rice

1 cup basmati rice
2 onions, roughly chopped
2 garlic cloves, roughly chopped
2 inch piece fresh ginger
1 teaspoon poppy seeds
8 peppercorns
1¼ cup plain yogurt
1 teaspoon garam masala
3 lb. oven-ready chicken
3 tablespoons ghee
½ teaspoon chili powder
½ cup sultanas
½ cup slivered almonds
1½ cups water
salt
sprigs of cilantro, to garnish

A chicken is stuffed with flavored basmati rice and cooked in the oven.

1 Place the rice in a bowl of cold water and leave to soak for 1 hour.
2 Place the onions, garlic, ginger, poppy seeds, peppercorns, and half the yogurt in a blender or food processor and work to a paste. Stir in the garam masala and add salt to taste.
3 Prick the chicken all over with a fork and rub in the blended mixture. Leave to stand for 1 hour. Drain the rice.
4 Heat 1 tablespoon of the ghee in a pan, add the rice and fry for 3 minutes, stirring constantly. Add the chili powder, sultanas, almonds, and salt to taste and stir well. Pour in the water and simmer for about 10 minutes, until the rice is almost tender and the water is absorbed. Leave to cool.
5 When the rice is cold, use it to stuff the chicken; sew up both ends. Place on a baking tray and cook in a preheated oven, 375°F for 1 hour 20 minutes, or until the juices run clear. If the chicken appears to be browning too quickly, place aluminum foil over the top.
6 Remove the chicken and allow to rest. Add the remaining yogurt to the juices in the tray and some water, if necessary, a spoonful at a time, stirring until it is all absorbed. Add more salt if necessary. Serve the chicken in joints or thick slices with the sauce, garnished with cilantro sprigs.

Serves 4
Preparation time: 15 minutes, plus soaking and marinating
Cooking time: 1 hour 15 minutes
Oven temperature: 375°F

Chicken Bhuna

3 tablespoons ghee
8 dried curry leaves
1 teaspoon black mustard seeds
1 large onion, chopped
4 garlic cloves, chopped
1 inch piece fresh ginger, chopped
1 tablespoon curry powder
1 teaspoon garam masala
1 teaspoon ground cumin
1 teaspoon ground coriander
2 teaspoons chili powder
1½ lb. skinless, boneless chicken
   breasts or thighs, cut into
   1 inch cubes
1 teaspoon salt
½ cup water

Serve this dry chicken curry with Indian flat breads, such as Chapati or Paratha (see pages 124 and 125).

1 Heat the ghee in a heavy-based frying pan, crumble the curry leaves and add them to the pan with the mustard seeds. Fry them over a gentle heat for 1 minute.
2 Place the onion, garlic, and ginger in a blender or food processor and blend to a coarse paste. Add this paste to the fried curry leaves and mustard seeds and cook gently for a further 5 minutes.
3 Add the curry powder, garam masala, cumin, ground coriander, and chili powder to the pan, and cook, stirring, for 2 minutes.
4 Add the chicken, salt and water. Stir to coat the chicken evenly in the spice mixture, then cover the pan and cook over a gentle heat, stirring occasionally, for 20 minutes, or until the chicken is tender.
5 Remove the lid, increase the heat and cook the curry for a further 3–5 minutes, until thick and dry. Taste and adjust the seasoning if necessary and serve the curry immediately.

Serves 4–6
Preparation time: 10 minutes
Cooking time: 30–35 minutes

Butter Chicken

1 Combine the marinade ingredients in a blender or food processor, and set aside for the flavors to infuse.

2 Put the chicken pieces into a bowl, add the vinegar, mixing well, and set aside for 1–2 hours. Spoon the marinade into the bowl containing the chicken and vinegar and mix well. Cover and refrigerate overnight or for up to 24 hours.

3 Transfer the chicken pieces and all the marinade to a roasting tin. Place in a preheated oven, 325°F, and bake for 20 minutes.

4 Meanwhile, make the sauce. Heat the ghee in a large frying pan or wok and stir-fry the cumin seeds for 1 minute. Add the onion and stir-fry until it is crisp and golden. Add the cream and garam masala and simmer gently.

5 As soon as the chicken is cooked, transfer it to the sauce in the frying pan or wok and mix well. Transfer to a warmed serving dish and serve immediately, sprinkled with chopped mixed herbs.

Serves 4

Preparation time: 10 minutes, plus marinating
Cooking time: 20 minutes
Oven temperature: 325°F

1½ lb. skinless, boneless chicken breasts, cubed
7 tablespoons vinegar
1 tablespoon chopped mixed herbs, to garnish

MARINADE:
2–6 garlic cloves
2 inch piece fresh ginger
2 tablespoons mild curry paste
1 tablespoon chopped cilantro
1–4 green chilies (optional)
1 teaspoon dried mint
⅓ cup plain yogurt
½ teaspoon salt

SAUCE:
6 tablespoons ghee
1 teaspoon white cumin seeds
1 teaspoon black cumin seeds
1 small onion, thinly sliced
7 tablespoons cream
1 tablespoon garam masala

"Patience is a dish of gold."
Kashmiri proverb

Bangalore Chicken Curry

3 tablespoons ghee or vegetable oil
2 onions, thinly sliced
6 garlic cloves, chopped
1 teaspoon turmeric
1½ teaspoons ground dhana jeera
1½ oz. cilantro leaves
3 large green chilies, deseeded, and
    chopped
3½ lb. chicken, cut into 8 pieces
½ cup chicken stock
1 cup coconut milk
1 tablespoon lemon juice
salt

TO GARNISH:
sprigs of cilantro
yellow chili, diced
boiled rice, to serve (optional)

This "green" curry from central southern India is made with a large quantity of cilantro and fresh green chilies.

1 Heat the ghee or oil in a large, heavy-based frying pan. Add the onions and fry over a medium heat, stirring frequently, for about 5 minutes, or until they are softened and golden.
2 Stir in the garlic, turmeric, and dhana jeera and cook, stirring, for a further 3 minutes.
3 Place the cilantro and green chilies in a blender or food processor and blend to a paste. Add this paste to the pan, reduce the heat to low and cook, stirring constantly, for a further 10 minutes.
4 Add the chicken pieces to the pan, turning them in the spice mixture to coat them evenly, then add the stock, coconut milk, and a little salt. Bring to the boil, then reduce the heat, cover and simmer, stirring and turning the chicken occasionally, for about 50 minutes, or until the juices run clear. Stir in the lemon juice; taste and adjust the amount of salt if necessary.
5 Transfer the cooked chicken pieces to a warmed serving dish and keep them warm. Increase the heat and boil the curry sauce for 5–8 minutes to thicken it. Pour it over the chicken and serve immediately, with boiled rice, if liked and garnished with coriander and diced chili.

Serves 4
Preparation time: 20 minutes
Cooking time: 1 hour 20 minutes

Balti Chicken

6 tablespoons vegetable oil
1 onion, chopped
½ teaspoon turmeric
1 teaspoon ground coriander
1 teaspoon ground cumin
1 teaspoon chili powder
2 tablespoons water
1½ lb. skinless, boneless chicken, cubed
2 lb. tomatoes, chopped
1 large green pepper, cored, deseeded, and cut into squares
4–6 garlic cloves, chopped
2 fresh green chilies, chopped
salt
Chapatis or Parathas, to serve (see pages 124–125)

1 Heat the oil in a large, heavy-based frying pan or wok, add the onion and fry until soft. Mix the turmeric, ground coriander, cumin, and chili powder in a small bowl with the water. Stir this spice mixture into the onion and cook until the liquid has dried up—about 3–4 minutes. Add the pieces of chicken and fry on all sides, then add the tomatoes and a pinch of salt to taste. Cover and cook for 15 minutes.
2 Add the green pepper, garlic, and chilies. Cook, uncovered, until all the tomato juices have evaporated and the chicken is cooked through. Serve hot with Parathas or Chapatis.

Serves 4–6
Preparation time: 20 minutes
Cooking time: 30–35 minutes

"A cracked pot will yet hold sugar."
Tamil proverb

Chicken & Yogurt Curry with Mint

1 onion, chopped
4 garlic cloves, crushed
2 tablespoons chopped fresh mint
1 tablespoon grated fresh ginger
3 tablespoons ghee
½ teaspoon saffron threads, infused
  in 2 tablespoons boiling water
  for 10 minutes
2 teaspoons garam masala
1 teaspoon chili powder
1½ lb. skinless, boneless chicken
  breasts
½ teaspoon salt
½ cup plain yogurt
6 oz. tomatoes, chopped
sprigs of mint, to garnish
steamed or boiled rice, to serve
  (optional)

1 Place the onion, garlic, mint leaves, and ginger in a blender or food processor and blend to a smooth paste.
2 Heat the ghee in a large, heavy-based pan, add the blended paste and fry gently for 5 minutes.
3 Add the saffron with its infused water, the garam masala, and chili powder and fry for a further 1 minute.
4 Cut each chicken breast into 3 pieces and add the pieces to the pan with the salt. Stir to coat the chicken in the spice mixture and cook for a further 5 minutes, to seal the chicken.
5 Add the yogurt and tomatoes, stir well, cover the pan and simmer gently for 15 minutes, until the chicken is cooked.
6 Remove the lid and simmer uncovered for 45 minutes more to thicken the sauce slightly. Taste the sauce and adjust the amount of salt, if necessary.
7 Transfer the curry to a warmed serving dish, garnish with mint sprigs and serve with steamed or boiled rice.

Serves 4–6
Preparation time: 15–20 minutes
Cooking time: 1 hour 10 minutes

Special Spiced Balti Chicken

1 Dry-roast the peppercorns, kalonji, and fennel seeds in a pan over a low heat for 3 minutes, until fragrant. Remove from the pan and grind to a powder, using an electric spice mill or a pestle and mortar.
2 Heat the oil in the pan, add the onion, ginger and garlic and fry, stirring, for 5 minutes, until soft. Add the ground spices, the garam masala, ground coriander, cumin, chili powder, and turmeric. Stir-fry for 3 minutes, then add the water, the coconut milk powder, lemon juice and ½ teaspoon salt. Bring to the boil, stirring, then add the cardamom pods, cinnamon, and bay leaf. Simmer, stirring occasionally, for 15–20 minutes, until a glaze forms on top of the liquid.
4 Add the pieces of chicken, the tomatoes, and sugar and stir. Cover and cook for 20 minutes, or until the chicken is cooked. Remove and discard the cinnamon stick and bay leaf and serve the balti hot.

Serves 4–6
Preparation time: 20 minutes
Cooking time: 50–60 minutes

½ teaspoon black peppercorns
½ teaspoon black onion seeds (kalonji)
½ teaspoon fennel seeds
2 tablespoons vegetable oil
1 onion, chopped
1 inch piece fresh ginger, crushed
1 garlic clove, crushed
1 tablespoon garam masala
1 teaspoon ground coriander
1 teaspoon ground cumin
1 teaspoon chili powder
1 teaspoon turmeric
1½ cup water
½ cup coconut milk powder
1 tablespoon lemon juice
6 cardamom pods, bruised
2 inch piece cinnamon stick
1 bay leaf
2 lb. skinless, boneless chicken thighs, cut into bite-sized pieces
4 ripe tomatoes, skinned, deseeded, and roughly chopped
¼ teaspoon sugar
salt

fish
& seafood

Fishing is practiced along the entire length of India's coastline and on virtually all of its many rivers. Few fishing craft are mechanized, so total catches are low and the annual per capita fish consumption is modest. Kerala in the south is the leading fishing state. The types of fish available in Indian rivers, lakes, and seas are different from those found in the colder European and North American waters. Many of the recipes in this section have therefore been adapted for fish not always found in India, but more commonly available elsewhere.

Kerala Shrimp Curry

2 tablespoons peanut oil
I onion, finely chopped
3 garlic cloves, crushed
I inch piece fresh ginger, peeled
    and cut into fine strips
¼ lb. tomatoes, roughly chopped
I scant cup coconut milk
½ teaspoon salt
juice of I lime
2 teaspoons sugar
20 large raw shrimp, about ¾ lb.
    total weight
I scallion, sliced into fine strips and
    fried, to garnish

SPICE MIXTURE:
3 tablespoons dried, unsweetened
    coconut, lightly toasted
6 small dried red chilies, roughly
    chopped
10 black peppercorns
I teaspoon cumin seeds
I teaspoon turmeric

Southern Indian curries like this one are traditionally fairly spicy—the spiciness coming from the number of dried chilies used in the recipe.

1 Grind the ingredients for the spice mixture to a fine powder, using an electric spice mill or a mortar and pestle.
2 Heat the peanut oil in a large heavy-based pan, add the onion, garlic, and ginger, and cook, stirring occasionally, for about 3 minutes, until softened.
3 Stir in the ground spice mixture and cook, stirring constantly, for a further 2 minutes.
4 Add the tomatoes, coconut milk, and season with salt, then simmer for 6–8 minutes to reduce the sauce and thicken it slightly.
5 Stir in the lime juice and sugar, then add the shrimp and simmer the curry gently for about 8 minutes, or until the shrimp have turned pink.
6 Transfer the curry to a warmed serving dish and scatter over the scallion. Serve immediately.

Serves 4
Preparation time: 10–15 minutes
Cooking time: 20–25 minutes

Fish Molee

½ lb. fillets of cod or any whitefish
½ teaspoon turmeric
1 teaspoon salt
2 tablespoons ghee or vegetable oil
1 onion, finely chopped
3 garlic cloves, crushed
1 tablespoon freshly grated ginger
1 tablespoon curry powder
2 fresh red chilies, quartered
   lengthwise and deseeded
1½ cup thick coconut milk

This mild curry, cooked in rich coconut milk, comes from southern India. A similar curry is made in Sri Lanka, where it is called "white curry."

1 Rub the fish fillets with the turmeric and salt and set them aside while you prepare the curry sauce.
2 Heat the ghee or oil in a heavy-based pan. Add the onion, garlic, and ginger and fry over a gentle heat for about 3 minutes, until softened.
3 Stir in the curry powder and chilies and cook, stirring constantly, for a further 2 minutes.
4 Add the coconut milk and bring to the boil, stirring constantly, then reduce the heat and simmer the sauce for about 5 minutes, or until it has thickened slightly.
5 Add the fish and cook gently for a further 6–8 minutes, or until the fish flakes when tested with the point of a knife. Taste and adjust the seasoning if necessary. Serve hot.

Serves 4
Preparation time: 10 minutes
Cooking time: 20 minutes

Shrimp Vindaloo

1 Mix together the dried chilies, malt vinegar, garlic, ginger, mustard seeds, and peppercorns in a bowl, then stir in the ground coriander, cumin, and turmeric.

2 Heat the vegetable oil in a heavy-based saucepan, stir in the spice mixture and cook over a gentle heat, stirring constantly, for 5 minutes. Add the water to the pan, stir well, then cover and simmer the sauce gently for 15 minutes.

3 Remove the lid from the pan, increase the heat and cook the sauce over a moderate heat for 5 minutes to reduce it to a thick, coating consistency.

4 Stir the salt, sugar, and shrimp into the sauce. Cook for 3 minutes, or until the shrimp are heated through. Serve immediately.

Serves 4

Preparation time: 10 minutes
Cooking time: 30 minutes

6 dried red chilies, deseeded, and chopped
½ cup distilled malt vinegar
6 garlic cloves, chopped
1 inch piece fresh ginger, grated
1 teaspoon mustard seeds, lightly crushed
20 black peppercorns, lightly crushed
1 tablespoon ground coriander
1 tablespoon ground cumin
1 teaspoon turmeric
2 tablespoons vegetable oil
1 cup water
1 teaspoon salt
1 tablespoon brown sugar
1 lb. cooked peeled shrimp

Steamed Tuna Curry in Banana Leaves

½ lb. fresh tuna steaks
juice of I lime
4 large pieces banana leaf

GREEN CURRY PASTE:
I tablespoon cumin seeds
2 tablespoons coriander seeds
3 large green chilies, deseeded, and
    chopped
2 tablespoons fresh mint leaves
2 inch piece fresh ginger, grated
4 garlic cloves, crushed
2 tablespoons sugar
½ teaspoon salt
½ cup dried unsweetened coconut
¼ cup malt vinegar

TO GARNISH:
lime wedges
fine strips of lemon rind
I red chili, cut into rings

This is a very fresh-tasting curry. If banana leaves are unavailable, wrap the tuna steaks in a double thickness of buttered wax paper for steaming.

1 Place the tuna steaks in a shallow, nonmetallic dish and pour over the lime juice. Cover and set aside to marinate while preparing the curry paste.
2 Place the cumin and coriander seeds in a blender or food processor and process briefly. Add the chilies, mint, ginger, and garlic, and work for 1 minute to produce a paste. Add the sugar, salt, coconut, and vinegar, and blend again until all the ingredients are thoroughly combined.
3 Lay the pieces of banana leaf (or buttered wax paper) on a flat surface. Remove the tuna from the lime juice and place a steak in the center of each banana leaf. Spread the green curry paste over the tuna, completely covering the fish. Wrap up the banana leaves to enclose the fish, and secure with wooden skewers.
4 Steam the fish over a pan of boiling water for 18–20 minutes, or until the fish flakes when tested with the point of a knife.
5 Garnish the steamed fish with lime wedges and chili rings.

Serves 4
Preparation time: 15 minutes
Cooking time: 20 minutes

Cook's Note
There are dozens of varieties of chili peppers. These range from mildly warm to blisteringly hot and can vary in length from ¼ inch to 12 inches. Fresh chilies should look bright and shiny, with no markings on the skin. To prepare chilies, always wear rubber gloves and work under cold running water to prevent irritating fumes from rising into your face. Pull off their stalks and cut them in half lengthwise. Whether or not you remove the seeds depends on your personal preference: seeds provide more heat.

Madras Fish Curry

1½ lb. skinless cod fillet (or any
  whitefish), cut into 4 inch
  pieces
1 teaspoon turmeric
½ teaspoon salt
1 tablespoon dried tamarind
1 cup boiling water
4 tablespoons peanut oil
8 curry leaves
2 teaspoons black onion seeds
  (kalonji)
2 onions, thinly sliced
2 large green chilies, deseeded, and
  thinly sliced
2 tablespoons Madras curry paste
4 small tomatoes, quartered
4 tablespoons chopped cilantro

TO SERVE: (OPTIONAL)
steamed rice
Naan bread (see page 122)

A hot curry with the added tartness of tamarind—a favorite ingredient in Indian fish curries.

1 Rub the cod fillet pieces with the turmeric and salt, and place in a shallow, nonmetallic dish.
2 Soak the tamarind in the boiling water for 10 minutes, then strain the pulp through a sieve set over a bowl, pressing it against the sieve to extract as much flavor from the pulp as possible. Discard the pulp and pour the tamarind liquid over the fish. Cover and marinate for 1 hour in the refrigerator.
3 Meanwhile, prepare the curry sauce. Heat the peanut oil in a heavy-based frying pan, add the curry leaves and black onion seeds and cook gently for 1 minute.
4 Stir in the sliced onions and chilies, then cook for a further 3 minutes, until softened but not browned. Stir in the curry paste and cook for a further 2 minutes.
5 Remove the fish from the tamarind liquid and set aside. Add the tamarind liquid to the pan of fried ingredients, with the tomatoes. Stir gently to mix, then simmer the sauce gently for 10 minutes.
6 Add the fish and cilantro to the pan, cover and cook for a further 8 minutes, or until the fish is just cooked through. Taste and adjust the seasoning if necessary and serve the curry hot, with steamed rice or Naan bread, if liked.

Serves 4
Preparation time: 25 minutes, plus marinating
Cooking time: 25 minutes

Cook's Note
The tamarind tree grows extensively throughout India. Its long fruit pods contain seeds surrounded by a sticky pulp, which produces the acidic flavoring widely used in Indian cooking. Tamarind is most usually available in the form of a rectangular block of compressed pulp and seeds; it requires soaking in hot water to extract the sour juice.

Balti Shrimp

1 Melt the ghee in a large heavy-based frying pan or wok, add the onion and ginger and fry gently for 4–5 minutes, or until the onion is soft, then add the garlic.
2 Meanwhile, in a small bowl mix the ground coriander, ginger, turmeric, cumin, and chili powder to a paste with the vinegar, then add this paste to the pan and stir-fry for a further 3 minutes.
3 Add the cooked shrimp with the pieces of pepper and turn gently with a wooden spoon until they are well coated with the spices. Add the water and the tomato paste and stir well. Bring to the boil, simmer for 1–2 minutes, then serve immediately, garnished with cilantro.

Serves 4
Preparation time: 10 minutes
Cooking time: 10–15 minutes

¼ cup ghee
1 small onion, sliced
1 inch piece fresh ginger, chopped
2 garlic cloves, sliced
2 teaspoons ground coriander
½ teaspoon ground ginger
1 teaspoon turmeric
½ teaspoon ground cumin
½ teaspoon chili powder
2 tablespoons vinegar
1 lb. cooked peeled shrimp
1 red or green pepper, cored, deseeded, and cut into squares
1 scant cup water
1 tablespoon tomato paste
chopped cilantro leaves, to garnish

Balti Seafood Curry

1–2 tablespoons vegetable oil
2 onions, finely chopped
2 garlic cloves, crushed
1 green pepper, cored, deseeded, and sliced
2 tablespoons curry powder
2 teaspoons chili powder
¼ cup flour
2 cups hot water
1 lb. whitefish fillets, skinned and cubed
¼ lb. cooked shelled mussels
¼ lb. cooked peeled shrimp
4 tomatoes, skinned, quartered and deseeded
salt and pepper
red chilies, cut into thin strips, to garnish
steamed or boiled rice, to serve (optional)

This is quite a hot curry, as it contains curry powder and chili powder.

1 Heat the oil in a large, heavy-based frying pan or wok, add the onions, garlic and green pepper and fry until soft but not brown. Add the curry powder, chili powder and flour and cook gently for about 2–3 minutes.
2 Gradually add the hot water, stirring constantly. Bring the mixture to the boil, lower the heat to a gentle simmer, then add the pieces of white fish and cook for 15 minutes.
3 Add the cooked mussels and shrimp and the tomatoes to the pan, season with salt and pepper to taste and simmer for a further 5 minutes.
4 Garnish with strips of chili and serve immediately with rice, if liked.

Serves 4–6
Preparation time: 20 minutes
Cooking time: 30 minutes

"Look in vain for yesterday's fish in the house of the otter."

Hindi proverb

Hot & Sour Shrimp

4 oz. dried tamarind
1 cup hot water
2 teaspoons sugar (optional)
2 green chilies
¼ cup cilantro leaves
2 garlic cloves
1 onion, roughly chopped
2 tablespoons vegetable oil
1 teaspoon fennel seeds
1 teaspoon chili powder
1 teaspoon salt
1 lb. large raw peeled shrimp

1 Soak the tamarind in the hot water for 30 minutes, then strain the pulp through a sieve set over a bowl, pressing it against the sieve to extract as much flavor from the pulp as possible. Discard the pulp and stir the sugar into the tamarind water if you do not like a sour curry. Set aside.
2 Put the chilies, cilantro, garlic, and onion in a blender or food processor and work to a paste.
3 Heat the oil in a pan. Add the fennel seeds and fry for 30 seconds. Add the prepared spice paste, chili powder, and salt and fry gently for 5 minutes, stirring occasionally. Add the tamarind water, stir well, bring to the boil, then simmer for 5 minutes.
4 Add the shrimp, cover and simmer for 10 minutes, or until cooked through and pink in color, stirring occasionally. Serve hot.

Serves 4
Preparation time: 15 minutes, plus soaking
Cooking time: 25 minutes

Vinegar Fish

1 teaspoon turmeric
1 teaspoon salt
1 lb. cod or any whitefish
3 tablespoons vegetable oil
2 onions, sliced
2–3 green chilies, thinly sliced
2 garlic cloves, crushed
1 inch piece fresh ginger, cut into
    fine strips
2 tablespoons white wine vinegar
4 tablespoons water
sprigs of cilantro, to garnish

1 Mix the turmeric and salt together on a plate. Coat the fish in the mixture, adding more turmeric and salt, if necessary.
2 Heat the oil in a large frying pan, add the fish and fry gently on both sides for 1–2 minutes. Lift out the fish and set aside on a plate.
3 Add the onions, chilies, garlic and ginger to the pan and fry, stirring, until golden. Stir in the vinegar and water. Return the fish to the pan, cover and cook gently for 5–6 minutes, or until it is cooked through.
4 Transfer the fish to a warmed serving dish and serve, garnished with cilantro sprigs.

Serves 4
Preparation time: 10 minutes
Cooking time: 15 minutes

Fish with Yogurt

Cod steaks are marinated in yogurt, then cooked in a fragrant paste.

1 Place the fish in a shallow, nonmetallic dish and sprinkle with the salt. Add the yogurt and leave the fish to marinate for about 1 hour, turning once or twice.

2 Heat 1 tablespoon of the oil in a pan, add 1 of the onions and fry until crisp. Place this, together with the remaining onion, the ginger, green chilies and garlic, in a blender or food processor and work to a smooth paste.

3 Heat the remaining oil in a large frying pan with a lid. Fry the fenugreek seeds for 30 seconds, then add the prepared paste and fry until it starts to brown. Now add the fish and yogurt. Stir carefully and spoon the mixture over the fish. Cover the pan and simmer for 5–10 minutes, or until cooked through; if drying too fast add 2 tablespoons of water; if too liquid, uncover and allow to dry out.

4 Transfer to a warmed serving dish and garnish with cilantro sprigs as desired.

Serves 4
Preparation time: 10 minutes, plus marinating
Cooking time: 15 minutes

2 lb. cod or other whitefish
1 teaspoon salt
⅓ cup plain yogurt
4 tablespoons vegetable oil
2 onions, finely sliced
1 inch piece fresh ginger, finely sliced
4 green chilies
2 garlic cloves
1 teaspoon fenugreek seeds
sprigs of cilantro, to garnish (optional)

Coconut Fish

2 tablespoons vegetable oil
4 green chilies, deseeded, and
    chopped
2 garlic cloves, finely chopped
1 inch piece fresh ginger, finely
    chopped
½ cup creamed coconut
2 lb. thick haddock fillets, skinned
    and cubed
8 tablespoons lemon juice
salt
TO GARNISH:
coconut shavings
fine strips of lemon rind

This simple fish curry is light and fresh, with the combination of ginger, coconut, and lemon juice resulting in an aromatic dish, full of flavor. It is also quick and simple to prepare.

1 Heat the oil in a large frying pan, add the chilies, garlic, and ginger and fry gently for 3 minutes. Add the creamed coconut and, when bubbling, add the pieces of fish and season with salt to taste. Stir well.
2 Cook for 3–4 minutes, stirring constantly and breaking up the fish as it cooks.
3 As soon as all the fish is cooked through, pour in the lemon juice, stir well and serve, garnished with coconut shavings and strips of lemon rind.

Serves 4
Preparation time: 10–15 minutes
Cooking time: 10 minutes

"A single stick upon the hearth does not burn."

Kashmiri proverb

vegetables

Since many Indians are vegetarian, over the years Indian cooks have created a great variety of ways of cooking everyday vegetables. Pulses—dried beans, split peas, and lentils—are a staple in India and help provide a large measure of the daily protein for families who eat meat only rarely or not at all. Some pulses can be hard to digest and are almost always cooked with seasonings that make the beans more digestible, such as ginger, asafetida, or turmeric.

Cauliflower Pachadi

¾ lb. cauliflower florets
½ cup buttermilk
1 teaspoon salt
3 tablespoons ghee
1 large onion, thinly sliced
2 garlic cloves, crushed
1 tablespoon freshly grated ginger
1 teaspoon mustard seeds
1 teaspoon black mustard seeds
1 teaspoon turmeric
¼ cup dried, unsweetened coconut
½ cup water
2 tablespoons chopped cilantro
pepper
whole green chilies, to garnish

This is a traditional dish from Kerala in southern India, in which cauliflower is marinated in buttermilk before cooking.

1 Place the cauliflower florets in a bowl with the buttermilk, salt, and some pepper. Mix well to combine the ingredients and set aside for 2 hours to allow the cauliflower to marinate.
2 Heat the ghee in a heavy-based pan, add the onion, garlic, and ginger and fry over a gentle heat, stirring occasionally, for about 8 minutes, until softened and lightly golden.
3 Add the mustard seeds, turmeric and coconut and cook for a further 3 minutes, stirring constantly.
4 Stir in the cauliflower with its buttermilk marinade and the water. Bring the curry to the boil, then reduce the heat, cover the pan and simmer gently for 12 minutes, or until the cauliflower is tender.
5 Remove the lid, adjust the seasoning to taste, if necessary, and stir in the chopped cilantro. Increase the heat and cook for a further 3–4 minutes to thicken the sauce. Garnish with whole chilies and serve hot as a vegetable accompaniment to other curries, or with steamed rice or Indian bread such as Naan (see page 122).

Serves 4
Preparation time: 10 minutes, plus marinating
Cooking time: 30 minutes

Mushroom Curry *pictured*

2 tablespoons ghee or vegetable oil
3 garlic cloves, crushed
1 teaspoon freshly grated ginger
6 scallions, sliced
1 tablespoon curry powder
½ teaspoon mustard seeds
½ lb. button mushrooms, halved
½ lb. flat mushrooms, such as
    portabellas, thickly sliced
1 teaspoon salt
1 teaspoon garam masala
½ cup thick coconut milk
2 tablespoons lemon juice
sprigs of cilantro, to garnish

1 Heat the ghee or oil in a heavy-based frying pan. Add the garlic, ginger, and scallions and fry over a gentle heat, stirring occasionally, for 2 minutes, or until softened.
2 Stir in the curry powder and mustard seeds and cook for a further 1 minute. Add the prepared mushrooms and the salt. Stir well to mix, then cook, covered, for another 5 minutes, stirring occasionally.
3 Add the garam masala and coconut milk and cook, uncovered, for a further 4–5 minutes, until the sauce has thickened slightly.
4 Stir in the lemon juice. Adjust the seasoning, if necessary, then serve immediately, garnished with cilantro sprigs.

Serves 4
Preparation time: 10–15 minutes
Cooking time: 15 minutes

Spinach Paneer

12 oz. young leaf spinach, washed
    and dried
2 tablespoons ghee
½ lb. paneer, cut into 1 inch cubes
1 large onion, chopped
2 garlic cloves, crushed
1 large green chili, deseeded, and
    chopped
1 tablespoon grated fresh ginger
1 teaspoon turmeric
1 teaspoon ground coriander
1 teaspoon chili powder
½ teaspoon ground cumin
½ teaspoon salt

Paneer is an Indian curd cheese available from Indian grocers. It is also quite easy to make at home; for instructions see page 141.

1 Steam the spinach over a pan of boiling water for 3–4 minutes, until it has wilted, then leave to cool. Place the spinach in a blender or food processor and work briefly to purée. Set aside.
2 Heat the ghee in a heavy-based pan, add the cubes of paneer and fry, turning occasionally, for 10 minutes, or until they are golden all over. Remove them from the pan and set aside.
3 Add the onion, garlic, chili, and ginger to the hot ghee and fry gently over a low heat, stirring constantly for 5 minutes, until softened. Stir in the turmeric, ground coriander, chili powder, and cumin and fry for a further minute.
4 Add the puréed spinach and salt, stir well to combine, cover the pan and simmer gently for 5 minutes.
5 Stir in the fried paneer and cook, covered, for a further 5 minutes. Adjust the seasoning, if necessary, and serve immediately.

Serves 4
Preparation time: 15 minutes
Cooking time: 30 minutes

Bombay Potatoes

4 tablespoons vegetable oil
½ quantity Curry Purée
     (see page 48)
1 tablespoon mild curry paste
2 tomatoes, thinly sliced
1½ lb. cooked new potatoes
Aromatic Salt (see Cook's Note)
1 tablespoon chopped mixed
     herbs, to garnish

Small new potatoes are perfect for this medium-hot curry.

1 Heat the oil in a large frying pan or wok and stir-fry the curry purée for 2–3 minutes. Add the curry paste and bring the mixture to simmering point. Add the sliced tomatoes.
2 When the sauce is simmering again, add the potatoes and stir gently until they are heated through. Season with aromatic salt to taste, sprinkle with the chopped mixed herbs and serve immediately.

Serves 4
Preparation time: 5 minutes
Cooking time: 10 minutes

Cook's Note
Spicy aromatic salt is widely used in Indian cooking, sprinkled over a variety of dishes. It is made by mixing dry-roasted spices (see page 50) with sea salt and grinding the mixture as finely or as coarsely as you wish, in an electric spice mill or using a mortar and pestle. Combine ¼ cup sea salt with 1 teaspoon each of dry-roasted coriander and cumin seeds, and ½ teaspoon each of dry-roasted szechuan pepper, fennel seeds, allspice, and sesame seeds. Store the aromatic salt in a small airtight jar in a cool, dry place, where it will keep indefinitely.

Spinach Bhajee

1 If you are using fresh spinach, wash it in cold water very thoroughly. Chop the leaves coarsely and boil them for 5 minutes in just the water clinging to the leaves. Strain, discarding the water. Frozen spinach should be defrosted and drained.

2 Heat the oil in a large frying pan or wok. Stir-fry the spices for 1 minute, then add the garlic and stir-fry for 1 minute more. Add the onion and stir-fry for 3 more minutes. Blend in the curry paste and bring the mixture to simmering point. Add the spinach and continue to cook, stirring frequently, until the spinach has heated through and the flavors have blended—about 5–7 minutes. Season with salt to taste and serve immediately.

Serves 4

Preparation time: 5–15 minutes
Cooking time: 15 minutes

1½ lb. fresh or frozen spinach
2 tablespoons vegetable oil
1–4 garlic cloves, chopped
1 large onion, chopped
1 tablespoon mild curry paste
salt

SPICES:
1 teaspoon white cumin seeds
1 teaspoon sesame seeds
1 teaspoon black mustard seeds
½ teaspoon black onion seeds
   (kalonji) (optional)

Mixed Vegetable Bhajee

1 Slice the vegetables into bite-sized pieces and blanch them briefly in a large saucepan of boiling water. Drain, refresh in cold water and drain again if you wish to prepare the bhajee at a later stage, or use the blanched vegetables hot straight away.

2 Heat the oil in a large frying pan or wok. Add the cumin, mustard and coriander seeds and stir-fry for 1 minute. Add the curry purée and stir-fry for 5–6 minutes more. Mix in the curry paste and the sliced tomatoes. When the mixture is bubbling, add the prepared vegetables, the chopped cilantro, and garam masala. Simmer until the vegetables are heated through and are as tender as you like. Season with salt to taste and serve immediately.

Serves 4

Preparation time: 15 minutes
Cooking time: 15–20 minutes

1½ lb. mixed vegetables,
   e.g. potatoes, carrots,
   cauliflower, celery, broccoli,
   baby corn
3 tablespoons vegetable oil
1 teaspoon white cumin seeds
1 teaspoon black mustard seeds
¼ teaspoon coriander seeds
1 quantity Curry Purée
   (see page 48)
1 tablespoon mild curry paste
3 tomatoes, thinly sliced
1 tablespoon chopped cilantro
2 teaspoons garam masala
salt

Yogurt Curry *pictured*

2 cups plain yogurt
2 tablespoons gram flour (besan)
2 tablespoons vegetable oil
½ teaspoon ground cumin
½ teaspoon ground coriander
2 garlic cloves, crushed
2 green chilies, finely chopped
2 red chilies, finely chopped
1 teaspoon turmeric
salt
1 tablespoon chopped cilantro
   leaves
6 curry leaves

TO GARNISH:
curry leaves
1 red chili, cut into rings

1 Mix the yogurt and gram flour together.
2 Heat the oil in a pan, add the cumin, ground coriander, garlic, and chilies and fry for 1 minute. Stir in the turmeric, then immediately pour in the yogurt mixture. Add salt to taste and simmer, uncovered, for 10 minutes, stirring occasionally.
3 Add the chopped cilantro and the curry leaves and continue cooking for a further 5 minutes.
4 Transfer to a warmed serving dish and serve, garnished with curry leaves and chili rings. Remove the curry leaves before eating.

Serves 4
Preparation time: 5 minutes
Cooking time: 20–25 minutes

Hyderabadi Eggplants

vegetable oil or mustard oil, for
   shallow-frying
1½ lb. eggplant, cut lengthways into
   quarters
4 oz. dried tamarind
2 large onions, sliced
1 teaspoon mustard seeds
½ cup ghee
1½ teaspoons ground coriander
1 fresh green chili, deseeded, and
   chopped
½ teaspoon chili powder
1 tablespoon dried, unsweetened
   coconut
3 garlic cloves, chopped
1 teaspoon turmeric
1 teaspoon garam masala
1 teaspoon sugar
3 bay leaves

1 Heat a little oil in a frying pan and fry the eggplant until the skins just turn crisp and brown. Remove and drain on paper towels.
2 Place the tamarind in a bowl with enough boiling water to cover and leave to soak.
3 Fry the onions and mustard seeds in the ghee in a large pan until brown, then add the ground coriander and green chili and fry for 5 minutes. Add the chili powder, coconut, garlic, turmeric, and garam masala and fry for 3 minutes further.
4 Strain the tamarind liquid through a sieve set over a bowl, pressing it against the sieve to extract as much flavor from the pulp as possible. Discard the pulp and add the tamarind liquid to the pan, with the sugar. Stir well and add the eggplant. Cover and cook for 10–15 minutes, until the eggplant is tender, stirring occasionally.
5 Fry the bay leaves in a little hot oil for a few seconds and pour over the eggplant just before serving.

Serves 4
Preparation time: 5 minutes
Cooking time: 20–25 minutes

Balti Mixed Vegetables

2–3 tablespoons vegetable oil
I small onion, chopped
I garlic clove, crushed
I inch piece fresh ginger, grated
I teaspoon chili powder
2 teaspoons ground coriander
½ teaspoon turmeric
I lb. diced mixed vegetables, e.g.
    potatoes, carrots, peas, beans,
    cauliflower
2–3 tomatoes, skinned and
    chopped, or 4 tablespoons
    lemon juice
salt
Naan bread or Chapatis, to serve
    (see pages 122 and 124)

1 Heat the oil in a large heavy-based frying pan or wok and gently fry the onion for 5–10 minutes, or until lightly browned. Add the garlic, ginger, chili powder, ground coriander, turmeric, and a pinch of salt. Fry for 2–3 minutes, then add the diced vegetables and stir-fry for a further 2–3 minutes.

2 Add either the chopped tomatoes or the lemon juice. Stir well and add a little water. Cover and cook gently for 10–12 minutes, or until the vegetables are tender, adding a little more water if necessary to prevent the vegetables from sticking to the bottom of the pan.

3 Serve immediately with Naan or Chapatis (see pages 122 and 124).

Serves 4
Preparation time: 15 minutes
Cooking time: 20–30 minutes

Balti Pumpkin

1 Soak the tamarind in the hot water for 15 minutes, then strain the pulp through a sieve set over a bowl, pressing it against the sieve to extract as much flavor from the pulp as possible. Discard the pulp and set aside the tamarind liquid.

2 Heat the oil in a large heavy-based frying pan or wok and fry the cumin, mustard, fenugreek and black onion seeds and aniseed for 30 seconds, then add the potatoes and fry for 2–3 minutes. Add the pumpkin, stir well and fry for 4–5 minutes.

3 Stir in the chili powder, turmeric, ground coriander, sugar and salt to taste and continue frying for 5–6 minutes. Add the tamarind liquid, cover and cook until the potatoes are tender, adding a little more water if necessary to prevent the mixture from sticking to the bottom of the pan. Serve hot.

Serves 4
Preparation time: 25 minutes
Cooking time: 25–30 minutes

¾ oz. dried tamarind
1 cup hot water
3 tablespoons vegetable oil
¼ teaspoon cumin seeds
¼ teaspoon mustard seeds
¼ teaspoon fenugreek seeds
¼ teaspoon black onion seeds (kalonji)
¼ teaspoon aniseed
3 potatoes, cut into chunks
1 lb. pumpkin (or other winter squash), cubed
1 teaspoon chili powder
½ teaspoon turmeric
1 teaspoon ground coriander
1 teaspoon sugar
salt

"A single ripe pear is better than a whole basketful of unripe pears."

Kashmiri proverb

Bengali Potatoes

1½ lb. small sweet potatoes, peeled
    and chopped
4 tablespoons sunflower or peanut
    oil
2 teaspoons panch phoran
    (see Cook's Note)
2–4 garlic cloves, chopped
1 large onion, chopped
1 tablespoon chopped cilantro
salt

This recipe uses sweet potatoes, which are ideal vegetables for spicy cooking.

1 Cook the sweet potatoes in a large pan of boiling water for about 15 minutes, or until soft.
2 Meanwhile, heat the oil in a large frying pan or wok and stir-fry the panch phoran spices for 1 minute. Add the garlic and stir-fry for 1 minute. Add the onion and stir-fry for 5 minutes more.
3 As soon as the sweet potatoes are cooked, strain them and add to the pan or wok with the chopped cilantro. Stir-fry until the ingredients are well blended and heated through. Season with salt to taste and serve immediately.

Serves 4
Preparation time: 10–15 minutes
Cooking time: 20 minutes

Cook's Note
Panch phoran is a Bengali five-spice mixture consisting of equal quantities of whole spices mixed together without dry-roasting or grinding. The mixture is used in one of two ways: it may be fried in oil to impart flavor to the oil before adding the main ingredients, or fried in ghee and stirred into cooked dhal or vegetable dishes just before they are served.

If panch phoran is unavailable, replace the 2 teaspoons of the spice in this recipe with ½ teaspoon white cumin seeds, ½ teaspoon fennel seeds, ½ teaspoon fenugreek seeds, ½ teaspoon black mustard seeds, and ½ teaspoon black onion seeds (kalonji).

Dhal

2 cups red lentils (masoor dhal)
1 cup water
1 teaspoon garlic powder
1 teaspoon ground cumin
1 teaspoon garam masala
dollop of ghee
salt
sprigs of parsley, to garnish

Although red lentils are specified in this recipe, any other types of lentils are suitable for making dhal.

1 Rinse the lentils in several changes of cold water. Place them in a bowl, cover with plenty of water and leave to soak for 30 minutes. Drain well.
2 Bring the measured water to the boil in a large pan. Add the drained soaked lentils. Cook, stirring occasionally until they reach simmering point. Cover the pan and cook for 20 minutes. The lentils should have absorbed the water, but will not yet be cooked.
3 Add the garlic powder, ground cumin, and garam masala and simmer the dhal for 10–15 minutes more, stirring occasionally to prevent it sticking. Stir in the ghee and season with salt to taste. Serve immediately, garnished with parsley sprigs.

Serves 4 as an accompaniment
Preparation time: 5 minutes, plus soaking
Cooking time: 35–40 minutes

Dhal with Fried Spices

This recipe involves heating oil or ghee until hot, adding spices and ingredients such as garlic, ginger, and onion, and sizzling the mixture until very hot. It is then poured directly over food in its serving dish.

1 Rinse the chickpeas and lentils separately in several changes of cold water. Still keeping them separate, soak them in plenty of cold water overnight to allow them to swell and soften.
2 Drain the chickpeas. Bring the measured water to the boil. Add the chickpeas and boil vigorously for 45 minutes. Drain the red lentils and add to the pan. Bring the water back to simmering point, stirring from time to time. Cover the pan and leave to simmer for 20 minutes. Stir the lentils to prevent them sticking to the pan. Add a little water if necessary and continue to simmer.
3 Meanwhile, heat the oil in a large frying pan or wok. Stir-fry the cumin and mustard seeds for 1 minute. Add the garlic and stir-fry for 1 minute. Add the onion and stir-fry for 5 minutes more. Blend in the curry paste. When the mixture is smooth, remove the pan from the heat. Taste the chickpeas and lentils to make sure they are cooked. Drain, if necessary, and transfer to a warmed serving dish. Add the fried mixture to the dhal and season with salt to taste. Serve hot, garnished with parsley sprigs.

Serves 4
Preparation time: 20 minutes, plus soaking
Cooking time: 1¼ hours

½ cup chickpeas
1½ cup red lentils (masoor dhal)
4 cups water
2 tablespoons vegetable oil
2 teaspoons white cumin seeds
2 teaspoons black mustard seeds
2–4 garlic cloves, finely chopped
1 large onion, thinly sliced
1 tablespoon mild curry paste
salt
sprigs of parsley, to garnish

"Men trip not on mountains; they stumble on stones."

Hindustani proverb

rice, chutneys, &breads

Rice or bread is always served as part of an Indian meal. Basmati rice, grown in the foothills of the Himalayan Mountains, is probably the most popular variety and has a distinctive and aromatic flavor. Most traditional Indian breads are unleavened. To enjoy them at their best they should be made just before the meal and eaten hot. A variety of accompaniments tend to be served with Indian meals, and particularly popular are yogurt relishes, which can be substantial dishes by themselves and provide a cooling contrast to spicy dishes.

Kitcheri

1½ cup long-grain rice
1½ cup red lentils (masoor dhal)
¼ cup butter
1 onion, chopped
1 garlic clove, chopped
2 inch piece cinnamon stick
5 cardamom pods
5 cloves
10 peppercorns
1½ cup boiling water
salt

A combination of rice and lentils that are cooked with cinnamon, cardamon pods, and whole cloves.

1 Wash the rice and lentils separately under running cold water, then leave to soak in fresh cold water for 30 minutes, still keeping them seperate.
2 Melt the butter in a large pan. Add the onion to the pan with the garlic, cinnamon stick, cardamoms, cloves, and peppercorns. Fry gently until the onion is soft.
3 Drain the rice and lentils and add the lentils to the pan. Fry gently, stirring, for 2 minutes. Add the water and salt to taste and simmer for about 10 minutes. Add the rice and simmer for 15–20 minutes, until the water is absorbed.
4 Transfer the rice mixture to a warmed serving dish, removing the cinnamon stick before serving.

Serves 4
Preparation time: 10 minutes, plus soaking
Cooking time: 30 minutes

"If rice is thrown on the roof, a thousand crows will come."

Tamil proverb

Coconut Rice

3 cups basmati rice
1½ cup thin coconut milk
½ teaspoon turmeric
8 shallots, roughly chopped
20 peppercorns
1 teaspoon salt
finely chopped scallions, to garnish

1 Wash the basmati rice thoroughly under cold running water, then leave to soak in cold water for 30 minutes; drain.
2 Put the coconut milk in a pan, stir in the turmeric, then add the drained soaked rice. Bring to the boil, then cover and simmer gently for about 10 minutes. Add the shallots, peppercorns, and salt and continue cooking gently for another 10 minutes or until the rice is tender. Be careful not to let the rice burn.
3 Transfer to a warmed serving dish and garnish with chopped scallions.

Serves 4
Preparation time: 35 minutes
Cooking time: 25 minutes

Saffron Rice

3 cups basmati rice
¼ cup butter or ghee
2 inch piece cinnamon stick
6 cardamom pods
6 cloves
1 onion, sliced
1 teaspoon saffron threads, infused
   in 2 tablespoons boiling water,
   for 10 minutes
1½ cup salted water

1 Wash the rice thoroughly under cold running water, then leave to soak in cold water for 30 minutes; drain.
2 Melt the butter or ghee in a large pan and fry the spices for a few seconds. Add the onion and fry, stirring, until golden. Add the drained soaked rice and fry for 2–3 minutes.
3 Add the saffron with its infused water and the measured water, stir and bring to the boil. Cover and cook gently for 20 minutes, or until the rice is tender and the liquid has been absorbed. Transfer to a warmed serving dish.

Serves 4
Preparation time: 35 minutes
Cooking time: 30 minutes

Parsee Pilau Rice

This rice dish goes particularly well with rich curries such as Lamb and Vegetable Curry (see page 46) or Chicken Bhuna (see page 70).

1 Heat the ghee in a large, heavy-based frying pan. Stir in the cardamom pods, cloves, cinnamon stick, and peppercorns and fry over a gentle heat, stirring constantly, for 2 minutes, until fragrant. Add the saffron threads and rice to the pan and fry, stirring constantly, for 1 further minute.

2 Add the salt, orange flower water, if using, and water. Stir well to mix. Bring to the boil, then reduce the heat, cover the pan and leave the rice to cook gently for 15 minutes without removing the lid.

3 Remove the pan from the heat and lightly loosen the rice grains with a fork. (All the water should have been absorbed.) Stir the sultanas into the rice, cover the pan with a clean, dry tea towel and allow the rice to cook in its own heat for a further 5 minutes.

4 Just before serving, stir the cashews and pistachios into the rice. Serve hot.

Serves 4–6
Preparation time: 10 minutes
Cooking time: 25 minutes

2 tablespoons ghee
6 cardamom pods, bruised
5 cloves
3 inch piece cinnamon stick, broken in half
¼ teaspoon black peppercorns, lightly crushed
¼ teaspoon saffron threads
3 cups basmati rice
¾ teaspoon salt
½ teaspoon orange flower water (optional)
2 cups water
¼ cup sultanas
¼ cup roasted cashew nuts
¼ cup pistachio nuts

Biryani

3½ cups basmati rice
8 tablespoons ghee or vegetable oil
4 inch piece cinnamon stick
8 cardamom pods
12 cloves
4 garlic cloves, crushed
1½ inch piece fresh ginger, chopped
1 teaspoon fennel seeds
½ teaspoon chili powder
2 lb. boned leg of lamb, cubed
1¼ cup plain yogurt
½ cup water
2 teaspoons salt
½ teaspoon saffron threads, infused
   in 3 tablespoons boiling water,
   for 10 minutes

TO GARNISH:
2 tablespoons ghee or oil
1 large onion, sliced
4 tablespoons flaked almonds
4 tablespoons sultanas

1 Wash the basmati rice thoroughly under cold running water, then leave to soak in cold water for 30 minutes.
2 Heat 6 tablespoons of the ghee or oil in a large pan. Add the cinnamon, cardamoms, and cloves and fry for a few seconds, stirring. When the spices have released their fragrance, stir in the garlic, ginger, fennel seeds, and chili powder. Fry for 5 minutes, stirring constantly.
3 Add the cubes of lamb and fry well on all sides. Stir in the yogurt a teaspoon at a time, allowing each spoonful to be absorbed before adding the next. Add the water and half the salt, cover and simmer for 40 minutes, or until the lamb is tender.
4 Meanwhile, fill another large pan two-thirds full with water and bring to the boil. Drain the soaking basmati rice and add to the pan with the remaining salt. Boil for 3 minutes, then drain.
5 Put the remaining ghee or oil in a large casserole, cover the base with some of the rice, and sprinkle with a little saffron water, then cover with a layer of the yogurt lamb. Repeat the layers, finishing with rice. Pour in any liquid from the lamb, cover closely with a foil-lined lid and cook in a preheated oven, 375°F, for 25–30 minutes, or until the rice is tender.
6 Meanwhile, prepare the garnish. Heat the ghee or oil in a small frying pan, add the onion and fry until golden. Remove from the pan and set aside. Add the almonds and sultanas to the pan and fry until the almonds are lightly browned and the sultanas plump.
7 Transfer the biryani to a warmed serving dish and sprinkle with the onion, almonds, and sultanas to serve.

Serves 4–6
Preparation time: 40 minutes
Cooking time: 1 ¼–1 ½ hours
Oven temperature: 375°F

"He who feeds on leaves knows not the flavor of fruit."

Tamil proverb

Cucumber and Mint Raita

¾ cup plain yogurt
1 cucumber, chopped
2 tablespoons chopped fresh mint
pinch of ground cumin
lemon juice, to taste
salt

This popular classic Indian accompaniment has a cool, refreshing flavor, which complements the heat of spicy dishes.

1 Place the yogurt, cucumber, mint, cumin, and lemon juice in a bowl. Add salt to taste and mix gently to combine.
2 Leave the raita to stand for 30 minutes before serving to allow the flavors to develop.

Serves 4
Preparation time: 10 minutes, plus standing

Banana and Coconut Raita

¾ cup plain yogurt
2 small bananas, thinly sliced
2 tablespoons dried, unsweetened
    coconut, toasted
pinch of chili powder
lemon juice, to taste
salt

1 Place the yogurt, bananas, coconut, chili powder, lemon juice, and a little salt in a bowl and mix gently to combine.
2 Taste and adjust the seasoning, if necessary. Serve the raita immediately as an accompaniment to curries.

Serves 4
Preparation time: 10 minutes

Eggplant Pickle

Some Indian grocers sell split mustard seeds, but if these are unavailable, use ordinary mustard seeds instead.

1 Place the cubed eggplant in a colander, sprinkle over the salt and set aside for 30 minutes, to allow the moisture to be drawn out of the eggplant.

2 Heat the oil in a large, heavy-based frying pan, add the turmeric, cumin, ground coriander, split mustard seeds and chili powder and fry over a gentle heat, stirring, for 3 minutes, until fragrant.

3 Add the ginger, garlic, chilies, and vinegar and stir well. Simmer gently for 10 minutes, stirring occasionally.

4 Add the drained eggplant cubes and the sugar to the pan. Mix well and cook over a moderate heat, stirring occasionally, for 35 minutes, or until the eggplant is very soft and all the flavors are well combined.

5 Ladle the eggplant pickle into sterilized jars, seal, and label. This pickle will keep well for 2–3 months.

Makes about 1¾ lb
Preparation time: 20 minutes, plus standing
Cooking time: 50 minutes

¾ lb. eggplant, cut into ½ inch cubes
1 tablespoon salt
⅓ cup vegetable oil
1 teaspoon turmeric
1 teaspoon ground cumin
1 teaspoon ground coriander
1 teaspoon split mustard seeds
1 tablespoon chili powder
2 inch piece fresh ginger, grated
4 garlic cloves, crushed
4 red chilies, deseeded, and thinly sliced
4 green chilies, deseeded, and thinly sliced
1 cup white wine vinegar
¾ cup soft brown sugar

Mango Chutney *pictured*

½ lb. dried mangoes, covered in cold water and soaked overnight
I teaspoon chili powder
6 cardamom pods, bruised
3 cloves
I teaspoon black mustard seeds
I teaspoon coriander seeds, lightly crushed
5 black peppercorns, lightly crushed
I small cinnamon stick, broken in half
¾ lb. fresh mango flesh, cut into ½ inch cubes
I large garlic clove, thinly sliced
½ teaspoon salt
I cup white wine vinegar
1½ cup sugar
poppadums, to serve (optional)

1 Drain the dried mangoes, reserving 1 cup of the soaking liquid, and cut the mangoes into ¾ inch pieces.
2 Place the chili powder, cardamom pods, cloves, mustard, and coriander seeds, peppercorns and cinnamon stick in a large, heavy-based frying pan. Dry-roast the spices over a gentle heat, stirring frequently, for 2–3 minutes, until fragrant.
3 Add the reserved mango soaking liquid, the dried and the fresh mango pieces, the garlic, salt, and vinegar to the spices in the pan. Bring the mixture to the boil, then reduce the heat and simmer gently for 10 minutes, stirring occasionally.
4 Add the sugar and stir over a gentle heat until it has dissolved. Increase the heat and boil the chutney, stirring frequently, until it is thick – this will take about 40 minutes.
5 Ladle the chutney into sterilized jars. Seal, label, and store for 2–3 months. Serve with poppadums or as an accompaniment to curries.

Makes about 2 lb
Preparation time: 20 minutes, plus soaking
Cooking time: 55 minutes

Pineapple Chutney

I large, ripe pineapple, peeled, cored and chopped into small pieces
3 shallots, chopped
I green chili, deseeded, and finely chopped
I tablespoon finely chopped fresh ginger
¼ cup raisins
¾ cup soft brown sugar
½ cup distilled malt vinegar
¼ teaspoon salt

1 Place the prepared pineapple with all the other ingredients in a heavy-based pan. Cook over a moderate heat, stirring constantly, until the sugar has dissolved. Bring the mixture to the boil, then reduce the heat a little and boil steadily for 8–10 minutes, stirring occasionally, until most of the liquid has evaporated and the chutney is thick.
2 Pour the hot chutney into sterilized jars. Seal, label, and store. Once opened, the chutney will keep well for 3–4 weeks in the refrigerator. Serve with poppadums or as an accompaniment to curries.

Makes about 15 oz
Preparation time: 10 minutes
Cooking time: 15 minutes

Eggplant Pickle

I large eggplant
I small onion, finely chopped
3 green chilies, finely chopped
½ inch piece fresh ginger, cut into
    fine strips
2 tablespoons thick coconut milk
½ teaspoon salt
4 tablespoons lemon juice

This pickle is not overly spicy, largely because of the addition of coconut milk. It makes a good accompaniment to spicy meat or vegetable dishes.

1 Place the whole eggplant on a baking sheet and cook in a preheated oven, 350°F, for 30 minutes, or until soft. Leave to cool slightly, then slit it open and scoop out the flesh into a bowl.
2 Mash the eggplant with a fork and mix in the remaining ingredients. Taste the pickle and adjust the seasoning. Serve chilled.

Serves 4
Preparation time: 10 minutes, plus chiling
Cooking time: 30 minutes
Oven temperature: 350°F

Naan

½ oz. fresh yeast
¼ teaspoon sugar
2 tablespoons warm water
I lb. self-rising flour
I teaspoon salt
½ cup tepid milk
½ cup plain yogurt, at room
    temperature
2 tablespoons melted ghee, butter
    or vegetable oil

TO GARNISH:
2–3 tablespoons melted ghee
I tablespoon poppy or sesame
    seeds

Naan bread is made with leavened flour and is probably the most popular of Indian breads.

1 Put the yeast in a small bowl with the sugar and warm water. Mix well until the yeast has dissolved, then leave in a warm place for 15 minutes, or until the mixture is frothy.
2 Sift the flour and salt into a large bowl. Make a well in the center and pour in the yeast mixture, the milk, yogurt, and melted ghee, butter or oil. Mix well to a smooth dough and turn on to a lightly floured surface. Knead well for about 10 minutes, until smooth and elastic. Place in the bowl, cover with a damp tea towel and leave to rise in a warm place for 1–1½ hours, or until doubled in size.
3 Turn the dough on to a lightly floured surface, knead for a few minutes, then divide it into 6 pieces. Pat each piece into a round.
4 Arrange on warmed baking sheets and cook in a preheated oven, 475°F, for 10 minutes. Brush with melted ghee or butter and sprinkle with the poppy or sesame seeds. Serve warm.

Makes 6
Preparation time: 30 minutes, plus standing and rising
Cooking time: 10 minutes
Oven temperature: 475°F

Puri

Like the Chapati (see page 124), the puri is made with ata flour but it is smaller—only 4 inches in diameter—and deep-fried, which makes the bread puff up. Serve them alone as a snack or as an accompaniment to curries.

2 cups ata or wholemeal flour
1 tablespoon ghee
1 cup warm water
vegetable oil, for deep-frying
Aromatic Salt (see page 100)

1 Place the flour, ghee, and water in a large bowl and mix to a soft dough. Knead for about 10 minutes, then leave it to stand for about 30 minutes.

2 Divide the dough into 16 pieces. With lightly oiled hands, shape each one into a ball and then roll out on a lightly oiled surface to make 4 inch circles.

3 Heat the oil in a deep pan to 375°F, or until a cube of bread browns in 30 seconds. Deep-fry the puris one at a time in the oil for 20 seconds, or until they puff up like balloons. Remove each one from the oil as soon as it is ready, sprinkle with aromatic salt and serve immediately.

Makes 16
Preparation time: 20 minutes, plus standing
Cooking time: 5–10 minutes

"If there be flour, cakes may be baked."

Tamil proverb

Chapati

2 cups ata or wholemeal flour
warm water, to mix
Aromatic Salt (see page 100)
melted butter, for brushing
    (optional)

The staple bread of northern and central India, the chapati is a very thin unleavened round bread, about 6 inches in diameter, made from fine-ground hard wholemeal flour (ata flour) and dry-cooked on a griddle or heavy-based frying pan.

1 Mix the flour in a large bowl with enough water to make a soft, pliable dough. Leave to stand for about 30 minutes.
2 Divide the dough into 8 pieces. Roll out each piece on a lightly floured surface to a circle about 7–8 inches in diameter.
3 Heat a large, heavy-based frying pan over a fairly high heat. Place the chapatis on the dry pan one at a time. After 20–30 seconds, characteristic dark blistering patches appear.
4 Turn the chapati over and cook the other side for about 30 seconds. Sprinkle with aromatic salt and brush with a little melted butter, as desired. Serve promptly or they cool and harden.

Makes 8
Preparation time: 10 minutes, plus standing
Cooking time: 8 minutes

Paratha

The paratha is a wholemeal bread, similar to the Chapati (see page 124), except that it contains ghee, which gives it a flaky texture. Parathas are thicker than chapatis and shallow-fried, as opposed to dry cooked.

2 cups plain wholemeal flour
1 teaspoon salt
about 1 cup water
1–1½ tablespoons melted ghee or
   vegetable oil

1 Mix the flour and salt in a large bowl with enough water to make a soft pliable dough. Knead for 10 minutes, then cover and leave to stand for about 30 minutes.

2 Knead the dough again, then divide into 6 pieces. Roll out each piece on a lightly floured surface into a thin round. Brush with melted ghee or oil and fold in half, brush the top with more ghee or oil and fold in half again. Carefully roll out again to a circle about ⅛ inch thick.

3 Lightly grease a griddle or heavy-based frying pan with a little ghee or oil and place over a moderate heat. Add a paratha and cook for 1 minute. Lightly brush the top with a little melted ghee or oil and turn over. Brush all round the edge with ghee or butter and cook until golden. Remove from the pan and keep warm while cooking the rest. Serve warm.

Makes 6
Preparation time: 30 minutes, plus standing
Cooking time: 15 minutes

desserts & drinks

Climate, local custom, and the availability of local products has affected the evolution of Indian sweets. Desserts from western and southern India, for example, feature coconut, while in the wheat-growing areas of the north there are more dishes made with flour and wheat products, such as semolina. Nowadays, everyday meals in India generally end with fresh fruit, which is refreshing, cleanses the palate, and makes a perfect conclusion to a spicy meal. Desserts and candies are usually reserved for festive occasions.

Indian Rice Pudding

¾ cup long-grain rice
6 cups milk
¼ cup sultanas (optional)
sugar, to taste
½ cup cream

TO DECORATE:
lightly crushed cardamom seeds
rose petals

This Indian variation on rice pudding, delicately flavored with sultanas and flaked almonds or pistachios, is absolutely wonderful.

1 Place the rice and 3½ cups of the milk in a heavy-based pan. Cook gently at simmering point for 45 minutes to 1 hour, until most of the milk has been absorbed.
2 Add the remaining milk and the sultanas, if using, stir well and continue simmering until thickened. Remove from the heat and add sugar to taste.
3 Leave until completely cold, stirring occasionally to prevent a skin forming, then stir in the cream.
4 Turn into small dishes and serve cold, sprinkled with crushed cardamom seeds and rose petals.

Serves 4
Preparation time: 5 minutes, plus chilling
Cooking time: about 1 hour

"The stomach pain is the greatest pain."

Kashmiri proverb

Semolina Barfi   *pictured*

½ cup fine semolina
½ cup granulated sugar
1½ cup milk
¼ cup butter
10 cardamom pods, peeled and
    crushed
¾ cup blanched almonds, halved
    and toasted

1 Place the semolina and sugar in a heavy-based pan and gradually stir in the milk until smooth. Add the butter in small pieces. Bring to the boil, stirring, then simmer for 3–4 minutes, until thickened, stirring occasionally to prevent sticking. Add the cardamom pods and continue cooking for another 10 minutes, until the mixture leaves the side of the pan.
2 Spread the mixture on a buttered plate or in a shallow dish to a thickness of ½–1 inch. Leave until almost cold, then decorate with the almonds.
3 Serve cold, cut into slices or squares.

Serves 4–6
Preparation time: 15 minutes, plus cooling
Cooking time: 20 minutes

Almond Barfi

2½ cups milk
¼ cup sugar
½ cup ground almonds
6 cardamom pods, peeled and
    crushed

In this imaginative milk pudding recipe, the milk is cooked very slowly until it becomes thick and lumpy, and is then flavored with sugar, ground almonds, and crushed cardamom pods.

1 Pour the milk into a large, heavy-based pan and cook for about 1¼ hours over a gentle heat, until it is reduced to a thick, lumpy consistency. Stir occasionally and be careful not to let the milk burn.
2 Stir in the sugar, then add the ground almonds and cook for 2 minutes. Pour the mixture into a buttered shallow dish and sprinkle with the crushed cardamom pods. Serve warm, cut into squares or diamond shapes.

Serves 4
Preparation time: 10 minutes
Cooking time: 1¼ hours

Yogurt Dessert

4 cups plain yogurt
¼ teaspoon saffron threads
about 2 tablespoons sugar
about 1 tablespoon rosewater

TO DECORATE:
1–2 teaspoons cardamom seeds,
    crushed
1 tablespoon pistachio nuts, shelled
    and chopped

This yogurt-based dessert is flavored with saffron and rosewater.

1 Turn the yogurt into a sieve lined with cheesecloth and leave to drip over a bowl for 6 hours. Put the dried curds—there should be about 1¼ cup—into a bowl and beat in the saffron. Add the sugar to taste—add a little more if you like, but it should not be too sweet.
2 Mix in the rosewater, a little at a time, until the mixture resembles thick cream. Cover and chill until required.
3 Spoon into individual bowls and decorate with the crushed cardamom seeds and chopped pistachios to serve.

Serves 4
Preparation time: 10 minutes, plus standing and chilling

Milk Dessert

3 pints whole milk
3–4 tablespoons sugar

TO DECORATE:
2 leaves varq (silver leaf)
edible flower petals

1 Cook the milk in a large, heavy-based pan for about 1¼ hours, until it is reduced to a thick, lumpy consistency. Stir occasionally and be careful not to let the milk burn.
2 Add the sugar and continue cooking for 10 minutes.
3 Spread the mixture on a lightly buttered plate—it should be a lightly cream colored, softly-set toffee.
4 Cut into wedges and serve cold, decorated with strips of varq and edible flower petals.

Serves 4–6
Preparation time: 5 minutes
Cooking time: 1 hour 25 minutes

Cook's Note
Varq is edible silver leaf, often used in Indian cooking for decorative purposes. Available from Indian food stores, it is very fragile and should be handled with care.

Almond Ice Cream

2 cups blanched almonds
6 cups milk
1 cup sugar
1 cup heavy cream
2 tablespoons rosewater

Milk, sugar, and cream are combined with ground almonds to produce a frozen dessert.

1 Place the almonds in a bowl, cover with cold water, and set aside. Reserve 1 cup of the milk and bring the rest to the boil in a large, heavy-based or nonstick pan. Simmer until the milk is reduced by half, stirring from time to time to ensure that any skin or solids that cling to the side of the pan are well mixed in.
2 Drain the almonds and place three-quarters of them in a blender or food processor with the reserved milk. Blend the mixture for a few seconds until the almonds are roughly ground; the mixture should be crunchy. Add the almond mixture and sugar to the pan of milk and continue simmering for another 10–20 minutes, stirring constantly. Remove the pan from the heat and leave to cool to room temperature, then place in the refrigerator until well chilled.
3 Roughly chop the remaining almonds and add them to the chilled milk mixture with the heavy cream and rosewater, stirring thoroughly so that the ingredients are well mixed. Pour into molds and freeze until solid.
4 Transfer to the refrigerator 20 minutes before serving, then turn out and serve.

Serves 8
Preparation time: 1 hour, plus chilling and freezing
Cooking time: about 40 minutes

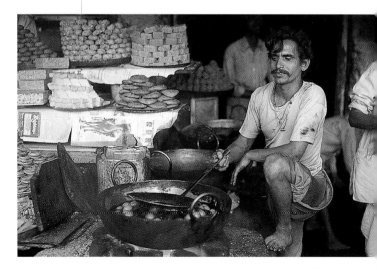

Mango Ice Cream *pictured*

13 oz. can condensed milk
1 cup heavy cream
½ cup granulated sugar
1 tablespoon roughly chopped almonds
1 tablespoon roughly chopped pistachio nuts, plus extra to decorate
13 oz. can mango slices or pulp, some reserved and chopped to decorate
1 tablespoon kewra water or lemon juice

1 Boil the milk and cream together in a large heavy-based pan with the sugar, stirring constantly until the sugar dissolves, then leave to simmer over a very low heat for about 30 minutes.
2 Stir in the almonds and pistachios, and cool to room temperature by standing the pan in a bowl of cold water.
3 If using mango slices, drain off half the juice from the can and crush the slices with the remaining juice. Reserve some to decorate.
4 Add the mango to the milk mixture, then add the kewra water or lemon juice and beat well. Pour into molds and freeze until the solid. Turn out, decorate with pistachios and mango and serve.

Serves 4
Preparation time: 20 minutes, plus freezing
Cooking time: 40 minutes

Cook's Note
Kewra water is an essence distilled from a palm-like plant called pandanus, and is available from good Indian grocers.

Pistachio Ice Cream

1 cup unsalted pistachio nuts, shelled, plus extra to decorate
13 oz. can condensed milk
1 cup heavy cream
½ cup sugar
2 eggs, separated
2 drops almond essence
2 drops green food coloring (optional)

1 Place the pistachios in a bowl, cover with cold water and set aside.
2 Heat the condensed milk in a pan and add the double cream and the sugar, stirring until the sugar dissolves. Beat the egg yolks into the mixture, together with the almond essence and the green coloring, if using, then leave the mixture to simmer gently.
3 Drain the pistachios and rub off the skins. Chop the nuts finely and add to the pan, beating in well. Bring to the boil, then leave to cool to room temperature. Place in the refrigerator until the mixture is nearly set.
4 Whisk the egg whites in a clean, nonmetallic bowl until they form peaks. Fold the beaten egg whites into the chilled mixture until evenly mixed, then pour into molds and freeze until firm. Turn out and serve decorated with chopped pistachio nuts.

Serves 4
Preparation time: 40 minutes, plus freezing
Cooking time: 15 minutes

Batter Coils in Syrup

3 cups all-purpose flour
⅔ cup plain yogurt
1 oz. dried yeast
2 cups granulated sugar
2 cups water
pinch of saffron
6 cardamom pods
6 cloves
vegetable oil, for deep-frying
icing sugar, to dust

1 Sift the flour into a bowl and add the yogurt, yeast, and enough cold water to form a batter the consistency of heavy cream. Cover and leave in a warm place for about 4 hours to ferment.

2 Dissolve the sugar in the water in a pan over a low heat with the saffron, cardamom pods, and cloves. Bring to the boil and cook to reduce the liquid and produce a heavy syrup. Set aside.

3 Heat the vegetable oil in a large pan to 350–375°F, or until a cube of bread browns in 30 seconds. Pour the batter in a steady stream through an icing bag, to form coil shapes in the hot oil below. Make a few coils at a time and cook for about 1 minute, turning, until they are light brown and crisp.

4 Remove the coils from the pan with a slotted spoon, drain on kitchen paper, then immerse in the syrup for about 5 minutes.

5 Remove them from the syrup; drain and dust with icing sugar. Serve immediately while warm and crisp.

Serves 4

Preparation time: 20 minutes, plus fermenting
Cooking time: 20 minutes

Sweet Lassi

A yogurt and milk drink that is blended with rosewater and ice cubes. Fruits, such as mango and banana, are often blended in.

1 Place the yogurt, milk, and kewra water or rosewater in a blender or food processor with sugar to taste. Add some ice cubes and blend until the ice cubes have almost disappeared.
2 Pour into tall glasses and serve immediately.

Serves 4
Preparation time: 5 minutes

1 cup plain yogurt
1 cup milk
½ teaspoon kewra water or
   rosewater
sugar
ice cubes

Salted Lassi

1 Place the cumin seeds in a heavy-based pan set over a fairly high heat and dry-roast for 1–2 minutes. Cool slightly, then grind using an electric spice mill or a pestle and mortar.
2 Place the yogurt, milk, lemon juice, dry-roasted and ground cumin, and salt into a blender or food processor. Add some ice cubes and blend briefly. Taste and add more salt if necessary, then pour into tall glasses and serve immediately.

Serves 4
Preparation time: 5 minutes
Cooking time: 1–2 minutes

1 teaspoon cumin seeds
1 cup plain yogurt
1 cup chilled milk
4 tablespoons lemon juice
½–1 teaspoon salt
ice cubes

"Where love reigns, the impossible may be attained."

Tamil proverb

Rice and Milk Dessert *pictured*

¼ cup basmati rice
½ cup water
2 cups milk
½ cup sugar
5 drops kewra water
¼ cup mixed pistachio nuts and almonds, chopped, plus extra to decorate

1 Soak the rice in a bowl containing the water for 1½ hours. Cook the rice in a large pan of boiling water for 15 minutes, then drain.
2 Heat the milk slowly in a pan and stir in the rice. Place the mixture in a blender or food processor and blend to a smooth paste. Return to the pan, heat gently and stir until the mixture begins to thicken. Remove from the heat and add the sugar.
3 When the sugar is fully dissolved, bring to the boil and simmer for 2 minutes. Leave to cool, then add the kewra water and the chopped pistachios and almonds.
4 Serve chilled, decorated with almonds and pistachios.

Serves 4
Preparation time: 10 minutes, plus soaking and chilling
Cooking time: 10–15 minutes

Carrot Halva

4 cups milk
1¼ cup carrot, finely grated
3 tablespoons butter
1 tablespoon golden syrup (or maple syrup)
½ cup granulated sugar
¼ cup sultanas or raisins
TO DECORATE:
1 teaspoon cardamom seeds, crushed
2 leaves varq (silver leaf)

1 Place the milk and grated carrot in a heavy-based pan and cook over a high heat, stirring occasionally, until the liquid has evaporated. Add the butter, syrup, sugar, and dried fruit. Stir until the butter and sugar have melted, then cook for 15–20 minutes, stirring frequently, until the mixture starts to leave the side of the pan.
2 Pour into a shallow buttered dish and spread evenly. Decorate with crushed cardamom seeds and strips of varq. Cut into slices and serve warm or cold.

Serves 4–6
Preparation time: 10 minutes
Cooking time: 45–50 minutes

glossary

ANISEED
Seeds of the anise plant, an aromatic plant that originated in India and Egypt. Aniseed has a licorice flavor and is often used in curries and marinades.

AROMATIC SALT
Used in a variety of dishes. Combine ¼ cup sea salt with 1 teaspoon each of dry-roasted coriander and cumin seeds, and ½ teaspoon each of dry-roasted szechuan pepper, fennel seeds, allspice, and sesame seeds. Grind as finely as desired. Store in a small airtight jar in a cool, dry place. Keeps indefinitely.

BASMATI
A special variety of Indian rice that has long grains and a distinctive flavor. It works particularly well in pilau dishes and in desserts. It should always be soaked in cold water for about 30 minutes before use.

CARDAMOM
Plant native to southwestern India; pods contain seeds that are dried and then ground. Most often used as a flavoring for rice and cakes.

CHICKPEA
Legume with rounded edible seeds enclosed in pods. If dried, chickpeas should always be soaked before use, but they are also available precooked and canned. Rich in carbohydrates, proteins, calcium, and iron.

CHILI POWDER
Varies in strength according to its country of origin. Indian chili powder is made from the dried and ground flesh and seeds of red chilies. It is similar to cayenne pepper.

CILANTRO
The fresh, bright green leaves of the coriander plant, frequently used as a garnish.

CINNAMON
Obtained by drying and rolling up the bark of cinnamon trees, cinnamon makes a tube that has a sweet aroma and a hot spicy flavor. It is also available in powder form.

CLOVES
Dried flower buds of the clove tree. Cloves are used in many meat dishes, as well as in marinades, pickles, and as an ingredient in spice mixtures.

COCONUT MILK
Widely used in Indian cookery, coconut milk can be made from scratch using either dried or fresh coconut, but it is also readily available canned in from supermarkets.

CORIANDER
Coriander has an intense flavor and aroma. The leaves (cilantro), roots, and seeds are all used in cooking.

CUMIN
The seeds of an aromatic plant, with a hot and slightly bitter taste. Cumin blends well with coriander and other spices. It is an ideal flavoring for fish and shrimp.

CURRY LEAVES
Not to be confused with curry powder, the dry spice blend, curry leaves come from a tree found in India and Sri Lanka. They may be used both fresh and dry, but are only included in dishes as a flavoring during cooking (much as bay leaves) and are removed before serving.

DHANA JEERA
A spice blend of coriander and cumin in a 1:1 ratio. Used in Southern India.

FENNEL SEEDS
Light greenish-brown in color, used widely in Indian cookery, particularly with meat, fish, and vegetables. Whole roasted fennel seeds are also chewed in India after a meal to freshen the palate.

FENUGREEK POWDER
The fenugreek plant is a member of the pea family. It produces long, slender pods that contain flattened brown seeds. These are roasted and ground and used as a flavoring in curries. It is also one of the main ingredients in curry powder.

GARAM MASALA
This is mild, sweet seasoning from northern India that is available in many supermarkets and Indian food stores. It usually contains cardamom, cinnamon, cloves, cumin, coriander, and black peppercorns.

GHEE
This is clarified butter that can be heated to higher temperatures than other oils, without burning. It can also be stored for a lot longer than butter. There are two types of ghee: pure (a dairy product) and vegetable ghee.

GINGER
Plant native to southeast Asia. Underground stems can be used fresh or powdered. Used in India to flavor

meat, fish, rice, vegetables, and curries, and to make tea.

GRAM FLOUR
Also called BESAN, gram is made from chickpeas and is used in Indian cooking to thicken sauces and to make various breads. It has a light golden color and a distinctive taste.

KALONJI
Black onion seeds, also called nigella seeds, impart a spicy onion flavor, often sprinkled over breads before baking. Available at Indian grocers.

LENTILS
Small, round dry seeds, always eaten shelled and cooked. They originated in central Asia and are a staple food in many countries.

MASOOR DHAL
Pinky-orange in color, called "red lentils." They should be cooked before being added to dishes, or they can be cooked with onion and spices as a dish on their own. Red lentils do not need to be soaked before cooking.

MINT
Fragrant herb with a strong fresh flavor and many varieties. It is used in many Indian dishes, especially with lamb.

MOONG DHAL
Small split yellow bean, very similar to lentils, having a green skin and yellow flesh. The beans are used in soups and are more popular in northern India than in the south.

OKRA
Tropical plant, rich in vitamin C, calcium, phosphorus, and iron. Available year-round for purchase fresh, frozen, or in cans. Popular in Indian cookery, it may be substituted for eggplant in any of the eggplant dishes.

ORANGE FLOWER WATER
A delicate flavoring, used in the same manner as rosewater.

PANCH PHORAN
Bengali five-spice mixture consisting of equal quantities of white cumin seeds, fennel seeds, fenugreek seeds, black mustard seeds, and black onion seeds (kalonji).

PANEER
Curd cheese. Available from Indian food stores, it is also quite easy to make at home. Simply boil 4½ cups milk over low heat. Remove from heat and add 2 tablespoons lemon juice, stirring continuously. The milk will thicken and curdle. Strain the curdled milk through a cheesecloth-lined sieve and set aside under a heavy weight for about 2 hours, pressing it into a half-inch thickness. Once set, paneer goes particularly well with vegetable dishes made with spinach or peas.

PAPRIKA
Spicy seasoning that is ground from a sweet pepper variety. Only small amounts of paprika should be bought at a time, as its flavor and color deteriorate quickly.

ROSEWATER
Used to flavor ice cream and pastries, it is available from the baking section of Indian markets.

SAFFRON
Dried stigmas of the saffron crocus, with a pungent smell and a slightly bitter flavor. It is the most expensive of all spices and is available ground or as whole threads. Many recipes require saffron threads to be infused in boiling water before use.

TURMERIC
In the same family as ginger and grows wild in countries in southern Asia. It has an attractive yellow color that is similar to saffron, and it is used both as a spice and a colorant Its flavor is more bitter than saffron.

TAMARIND
Fruit of a West African evergreen tree, the pods are brown, long, and wide and contain a pulp with a few hard seeds in it. In Indian cuisine, the pulp of dried tamarind is a major sour ingredient in many spice mixtures and is also used in chutneys.

VARQ
Edible silver leaf, used for decorative purposes. Quite fragile, it should be handled with great care. Available from Indian food stores.

index

a

almonds
    almond barfi 130
    almond ice cream 133
    chicken korma 58
    chicken stuffed with rice 68
    lamb with almonds 39
    lamb korma 40
    spiced roast lamb 36
aniseed 140
aromatic salt 100, 140

b

balti, special spiced chicken 77
balti beef 52
balti chicken 74
balti mixed vegetables 104
balti shrimp 87
balti pumpkin 105
balti seafood curry 88
banana and coconut raita 118
Bangalore chicken curry 72
barfi 130
basmati 140
batter coils in syrup 136
beef
    balti beef 52
    beef with coconut milk 32
    beef curry with potatoes 31
    beef with fenugreek 48
    beef and mango curry 49
    Calcutta beef curry 52
    chili fry 23
    meat samosas 19
    mince with potatoes and
      peas 28
    spicy beef curry 45
    stuffed eggplant 30
    stuffed peppers 20
Bengali panch phoran 106, 141
Bengali potatoes 106
besan flour, see gram flour
bhajees 101
biryani 116
Bombay potatoes 100
breads 122-5
butter chicken 71

c

cabbage leaves, stuffed 22
Calcutta beef curry 52
cardamom 140
carrot halva 138
cauliflower pachadi 96
chapati 124
cheese, spinach paneer 98
chicken
    balti chicken 74
    Bangalore chicken curry 72
    butter chicken 71
    chicken & yogurt curry with
      mint 76
    chicken bhuma 70
    chicken curry 63
    chicken and dhal curry 66
    chicken jalfrezi 59
    chicken korma 58
    chicken makhani 60
    chicken with spinach 64
    chicken stuffed with rice 68
    chicken tikka 24
    chicken tikka masala 56
    chili chicken 59
    Kashmiri chicken 62
    special spiced balti 77
    tandoori chicken 67
chickpeas
    dhal with fried spices 109
    lamb & vegetable curry 46
chili chicken 59
chili fry 23
chili peppers, preparing 84
chili powder 140
chilies
    eggplant pickle 119
    balti beef 52
    coconut fish 92
    Goan vindaloo 50
    shrimp vindaloo 83
    spiced scrambled eggs 16
    yogurt curry 102
chutneys 120
cilantro
    Bangalore chicken curry 72
    spiced scrambled eggs 16
cinnamon 140
cloves 140
coconut
    banana & coconut raita 118
    coconut fish 92
    coconut rice 114
    green curry paste 84
coconut milk
    Bangalore chicken curry 72
    beef with coconut milk 32
    coconut milk with beef 32
    fish molee 82
    Kerala shrimp curry 80
    lamb korma 40
    mushroom curry 98
cucumber and mint raita 118

cumin 140
curries
    fish 80, 82-6, 88, 92
    meat 31, 35, 38, 40-50, 52, 63,
      66, 70, 72, 76
    vegetable 98, 100, 102
curry leaves 140
curry pastes 45, 84
curry purée 48

d

dhal 66, 108
dhal and chicken curry 66
dhal with fried spices 109
dhana jeera 72
dry frying spices 50
dry pork curry 38
dry spice mixture 46

e

eggplant
    eggplant pickle 119, 122
    Hyderabadi eggplant 102
    lamb & vegetable curry 46
    stuffed eggplant 30
eggs, spiced scrambled 16

f

fennel seeds 140
fenugreek 48
fenugreek, with beef 48
fish
    coconut fish 92
    fish molee 82
    fish with yogurt 91
    Madras fish curry 86
    vinegar fish 90
fried spices with dhal 109

g

garam masala 28
ghee 40
ginger, spiced roast lamb 36
Goan lamb and pork curry 42
Goan vindaloo 50
gram flour 14, 140
green curry paste 84

h

halva, carrot 138
hot & sour shrimp 90
Hyderabadi eggplant 102

i

ice creams 133, 134
Indian rice pudding 128

k

Kashmiri chicken 62
Kashmiri kofta curry 41
kebabs 17, 34
Kerala shrimp curry 80
kitcheri 112

l

lamb
    biryani 116
    Goan lamb & pork curry 42
    Kashmiri kofta curry 41
    lamb & vegetable curry 46
    lamb with almonds 39
    lamb kebab 17, 34
    lamb korma 40
    lamb tikka masala 44
    lamb with yogurt 51
    spiced roast lamb 36
    stuffed cabbage leaves 22
lassi 137
lentils
    chicken and dhal curry 66
    dhal 66, 108
    dhal with fried spices 109
    gram flour 14, 140
    kitcheri 112
    lamb & vegetable curry 46

m

Madras fish curry 86
mango and beef curry 49
mango chutney 120
mango ice cream 134
marinades 24, 40, 45, 56, 58, 60, 71, 96
masala mixture 46
masala sauce 44, 56
Masoor dhal 66
meat samosas 19
meatball curry 41
methi 48
milk dessert 132
milk and rice dessert 138
mint 141
mint, chicken & yogurt curry 76
mint and cucumber raita 118
mixed vegetable bhajee 101
mixed vegetables balti 104
moong dhal 141

moong dhal, lamb and vegetable curry 46
mung beans 141
mushroom curry 98
mussels, balti seafood curry 88

n

naan 122

o

okra 141
onions, lamb with yogurt 51
orange flower water 141

p

pachadi, cauliflower 96
Pakora 14
panch phoran 106, 141
paneer 98, 141
paprika 141
paratha 125
Parsee pilau rice 115
pastry, samosas 18, 19
peas
    stew with potatoes 28
    vegetable samosas 18
peppers
    balti beef 52
    balti chicken 74
    balti shrimp 87
    balti seafood curry 88
    chicken jalfrezi 59
    chili fry 23
    lamb kebab 34
    stuffed peppers 20
pickles 119, 122
pilau rice 115
pineapple chutney 120
pistachio ice cream 134
pork
    dry pork curry 38
    Goan lamb & pork curry 42
    Goan vindaloo 50
    pork vindaloo 35
potatoes
    balti pumpkin 105
    beef curry with 31
    Bombay potatoes 100
    lamb & vegetable curry 46
    mince with potatoes & peas 28
    pakora 14
    vegetable samosas 18
pumpkin
    balti pumpkin 105
    lamb & vegetable curry 46

puri 123

r

raitas 118
rice
    biryani 116
    chicken stuffed with 68
    coconut rice 114
    Indian rice pudding 128
    kitcheri 112
    Parsee pilau rice 115
    rice and milk dessert 138
    saffron rice 114
    stuffed cabbage leaves 22
    stuffed peppers 20
roast lamb, spiced 36
rosewater 141

s

saffron 141
saffron, lamb korma 40
saffron rice 114
salt, aromatic 100
salted lassi 137
samosas 18, 19
sauces 44, 56, 60, 71
scrambled eggs, spiced 16
seafood curry, balti 88
semolina barfi 130
shallots, coconut rice 114
shrimp
    balti shrimp 87
    balti seafood curry 88
    hot & sour shrimp 90
    Kerala shrimp curry 80
    shrimp vindaloo 83
    sour and hot shrimp 90
special spiced balti chicken 77
spice mixtures 28, 40, 42, 80, 106
spiced balti chicken 77
spiced roast lamb 36
spiced scrambled eggs 16
spices, dry fried 50
spicy beef curry 45
spinach
    chicken with spinach 64
    lamb & vegetable curry 46
    pakora 14
    spinach bhajee 101
    spinach paneer 98
spit roasted chicken 67
spring onions, mushroom curry 98
steamed tuna curry in banana leaves 84
stew with potatoes and peas 28